THE WAR ON DRUGS

Opposing Viewpoints®

OTHER BOOKS OF RELATED INTEREST

OPPOSING VIEWPOINTS SERIES

Alcohol
America's Prisons
Chemical Dependency
Civil Liberties
Crime and Criminals
Criminal Justice
The Death Penalty
Gangs
Gun Control
Juvenile Crime
The Legal System
Tobacco and Smoking
Violence
The War on Drugs

CURRENT CONTROVERSIES SERIES

Alcoholism
Crime
Drug Trafficking
Gun Control
Illegal Drugs
Police Brutality
Smoking
Teen Addiction
Youth Violence

AT ISSUE SERIES

Does Capital Punishment Deter Crime?
The Jury System
Legalizing Drugs
Smoking
Policing the Police

THE WAR ON DRUGS

Opposing Viewpoints®

David L. Bender, *Publisher*

Bruno Leone, *Executive Editor*

Bonnie Szumski, *Editorial Director*

Brenda Stalcup, *Managing Editor*

Scott Barbour, *Senior Editor*

Stephen P. Thompson, *Book Editor*

OPPOSING
VIEWPOINTS®
SERIES

Greenhaven Press, Inc., San Diego, California

Cover photo: MetaTools; Photodisc

Library of Congress Cataloging-in-Publication Data
The war on drugs : opposing viewpoints / Stephen P. Thompson, book
  editor.
      p.   cm. — (Opposing viewpoints series)
    Includes bibliographical references and index.
    ISBN 1-56510-805-1 (lib. bdg. : alk. paper). —
  ISBN 1-56510-804-3 (pbk. : alk. paper)
    1. Narcotics, Control of—United States. 2. Drug abuse—United
  States—Prevention. 3. Drug legalization—United States. I. Thompson,
  Stephen P., 1953–   . II. Series: Opposing viewpoints series
  (Unnumbered)
  HV5825.W381284 1998
  363.4'5'0973—dc21   97-52384
                                                                     CIP

Greenhaven Press, Inc., P.O. Box 289009
San Diego, CA 92198-9009

"CONGRESS SHALL MAKE NO LAW...ABRIDGING THE FREEDOM OF SPEECH, OR OF THE PRESS."

First Amendment to the U.S. Constitution

The basic foundation of our democracy is the First Amendment guarantee of freedom of expression. The Opposing Viewpoints Series is dedicated to the concept of this basic freedom and the idea that it is more important to practice it than to enshrine it.

CONTENTS

WHY CONSIDER OPPOSING VIEWPOINTS?

"The only way in which a human being can make some approach to knowing the whole of a subject is by hearing what can be said about it by persons of every variety of opinion and studying all modes in which it can be looked at by every character of mind. No wise man ever acquired his wisdom in any mode but this."

John Stuart Mill

In our media-intensive culture it is not difficult to find differing opinions. Thousands of newspapers and magazines and dozens of radio and television talk shows resound with differing points of view. The difficulty lies in deciding which opinion to agree with and which "experts" seem the most credible. The more inundated we become with differing opinions and claims, the more essential it is to hone critical reading and thinking skills to evaluate these ideas. Opposing Viewpoints books address this problem directly by presenting stimulating debates that can be used to enhance and teach these skills. The varied opinions contained in each book examine many different aspects of a single issue. While examining these conveniently edited opposing views, readers can develop critical thinking skills such as the ability to compare and contrast authors' credibility, facts, argumentation styles, use of persuasive techniques, and other stylistic tools. In short, the Opposing Viewpoints Series is an ideal way to attain the higher-level thinking and reading skills so essential in a culture of diverse and contradictory opinions.

In addition to providing a tool for critical thinking, Opposing Viewpoints books challenge readers to question their own strongly held opinions and assumptions. Most people form their opinions on the basis of upbringing, peer pressure, and personal, cultural, or professional bias. By reading carefully balanced opposing views, readers must directly confront new ideas as well as the opinions of those with whom they disagree. This is not to simplistically argue that everyone who reads opposing views will—or should—change his or her opinion. Instead, the series enhances readers' understanding of their own views by encouraging confrontation with opposing ideas. Careful examination of others' views can lead to the readers' understanding of the logical inconsistencies in their own opinions, perspective on why they hold an opinion, and the consideration of the possibility that their opinion requires further evaluation.

EVALUATING OTHER OPINIONS

To ensure that this type of examination occurs, Opposing Viewpoints books present all types of opinions. Prominent spokespeople on different sides of each issue as well as well-known professionals from many disciplines challenge the reader. An additional goal of the series is to provide a forum for other, less known, or even unpopular viewpoints. The opinion of an ordinary person who has had to make the decision to cut off life support from a terminally ill relative, for example, may be just as valuable and provide just as much insight as a medical ethicist's professional opinion. The editors have two additional purposes in including these less known views. One, the editors encourage readers to respect others' opinions—even when not enhanced by professional credibility. It is only by reading or listening to and objectively evaluating others' ideas that one can determine whether they are worthy of consideration. Two, the inclusion of such viewpoints encourages the important critical thinking skill of objectively evaluating an author's credentials and bias. This evaluation will illuminate an author's reasons for taking a particular stance on an issue and will aid in readers' evaluation of the author's ideas.

As series editors of the Opposing Viewpoints Series, it is our hope that these books will give readers a deeper understanding of the issues debated and an appreciation of the complexity of even seemingly simple issues when good and honest people disagree. This awareness is particularly important in a democratic society such as ours in which people enter into public debate to determine the common good. Those with whom one disagrees should not be regarded as enemies but rather as people whose views deserve careful examination and may shed light on one's own.

Thomas Jefferson once said that "difference of opinion leads to inquiry, and inquiry to truth." Jefferson, a broadly educated man, argued that "if a nation expects to be ignorant and free . . . it expects what never was and never will be." As individuals and as a nation, it is imperative that we consider the opinions of others and examine them with skill and discernment. The Opposing Viewpoints Series is intended to help readers achieve this goal.

David L. Bender & Bruno Leone,
Series Editors

Greenhaven Press anthologies primarily consist of previously published material taken from a variety of sources, including periodicals, books, scholarly journals, newspapers, government documents, and position papers from private and public organizations. These original sources are often edited for length and to ensure their accessibility for a young adult audience. The anthology editors also change the original titles of these works in order to clearly present the main thesis of each viewpoint and to explicitly indicate the opinion presented in the viewpoint. These alterations are made in consideration of both the reading and comprehension levels of a young adult audience. Every effort is made to ensure that Greenhaven Press accurately reflects the original intent of the authors included in this anthology.

INTRODUCTION

"Drug abuse is a serious problem, both for individual citizens and society at large, but the 'war on drugs' has made matters worse."
—Ethan A. Nadelmann

"The drug war is not being lost. In 1979, some 25 million had tried drugs sometime in the preceding month. Today that figure is 11 million. Why? Because of stricter drug laws."
—Mortimer B. Zuckerman

The war on drugs is never far from the front pages of America's newspapers and magazines. Recent newsworthy events include an intense debate over legalizing marijuana as medicine, a study showing a significant increase in teenage drug use since 1992, and a leading conservative journal's call for the legalization of drugs. But the war on drugs in the United States is more than just headlines; it is an expanding enterprise deeply embedded in the political and social fabric of the country, an effort that involves law enforcement, the legal system, education, health care, and a host of political and advocacy groups. Although it pervades society more than ever before, the war on drugs has also been subjected to increasing criticism in recent years. In one form or another, all the viewpoints collected in this volume address the constantly recurring question, "Is the war on drugs succeeding?"

The federal government's allocation for spending on the war on drugs for fiscal year 1998 was $16.0 billion. This total reflects a steadily growing budget, up from $2.7 billion in 1985. Where does all this money go? Of this total, $10.5 billion is designated for measures to reduce the supply of drugs, primarily through law enforcement efforts such as the interdiction of drug supplies at the nation's borders. Consistent with the trend since the mid-1980s, the law enforcement allocation is approximately double the funds provided to efforts to reduce the demand for drugs, which include drug treatment and education programs.

Supporters of current policies claim the war on drugs is succeeding, as evidenced by the steady decline in the overall number of illegal drug users since the late 1970s. Credit for this decline should be given, they maintain, to such anti-drug efforts as Nancy Reagan's "Just Say No" campaign of the 1980s and the school-based Drug Abuse Resistance Education (DARE) program. Supporters of the current policy also measure success by noting the vastly increased numbers of drug offenders in federal and state prisons. In this view, the steady increases in spending on the war on drugs are necessary to maintain the level of success achieved so far. If more sellers and users are in jail, supporters contend, then drug use will decrease and the spread of drugs will be contained. Advocates of the current policies argue that there is no valid alternative to the current form of fighting the war on drugs; abandoning these measures would lead to huge increases in drug use and abuse, along with a host of attendant social problems. Barry R. McCaffrey, director of the Office of National Drug Control Policy, asserts that, since 1990, "illegal drug abuse has cost America more than $300 billion and 100,000 dead." McCaffrey and other advocates of the current war on drugs insist that these figures would be much worse if the current approach were scaled back or abandoned.

The many critics of the war on drugs question the accomplishments of this mushrooming effort. Advocates of reform in the war on drugs fall into two broad groups: those who believe that progress can be made in the war on drugs by shifting priorities and modifying current policies, and those who believe the war on drugs has failed in its objectives and should be abandoned in favor of some form of drug legalization. Those in the first group of critics generally agree that treatment of drug abusers is more effective and cost-efficient than law enforcement approaches in reducing both drug abuse and crime. For example, scholar Jonathan P. Caulkins cites a study by the RAND Drug Policy Research Center estimating "that every dollar spent treating heavy cocaine users averts more than $7 in measurable social costs (criminal justice budgets, lost worker productivity, health care expenditures, etc.)." Moreover, these reformers believe that the increased incarceration of drug offenders is actually a sign that the war on drugs has failed. They claim that nearly 50 percent of the million Americans in jail are there for drug law violations. A country that locks up such a large percentage of its population, at such dramatic costs to families and taxpayers, is one with misguided priorities, critics assert.

Many opponents advocate legalization as an alternative to the current war on drugs. Supporters of legalization suggest that drug use is much less dangerous than the government wants people to believe. The health problems and deaths associated with drug use are minor compared to those associated with tobacco and alcohol use, they claim. Using a cost-and-benefit approach to the problem, they argue that legalizing drug use, with some age and use restrictions, would benefit society by freeing up police to fight more serious crimes, reducing the load on the overburdened courts, and creating prison space for more serious offenders. Advocates of legalization concede that some increase in drug use and abuse would result from legalization, but they contend the many benefits outweigh the costs.

However, opponents of drug legalization have public opinion on their side, according to recent surveys. Most Americans remain skeptical that such a radical change in the nation's drug laws is warranted. Critics of legalization contend that the first result of legalization would be a significant increase in the use and abuse of drugs. "Legalization," physician Robert L. DuPont argues, "will likely lead to increases in drug use, addiction and drug-related death." Opponents concede that legalization would reduce the burden on the criminal justice system, but they maintain that increased costs in health care and decreased job productivity would more than offset any potential benefits.

The War on Drugs: Opposing Viewpoints presents a wide variety of viewpoints about the current battle against drugs in the United States. Law enforcement officials, politicians, scholars, doctors, patients, and activists debate the following questions: Is the War on Drugs Succeeding? Which Current Policies Are Working in the War on Drugs? Is Legalization a Realistic Alternative to the War on Drugs? Should Marijuana Be Legalized for Medical Purposes? and What New Initiatives Might Impact the War on Drugs? Contributors express widely divergent opinions about current trends and potential tactics in the war on drugs.

CHAPTER 1

IS THE WAR ON DRUGS SUCCEEDING?

CHAPTER PREFACE

The war on drugs that is being waged by federal and local governments is more extensive and better-funded than ever before. While supporters of the effort are able to point to evidence of steady progress, critics point to different evidence that shows, in their view, that the drug war creates more problems than it solves. How can one determine whether or not the war on drugs is successful?

Because the overall rate of drug use has declined since 1979, and because the rates of crimes associated with drug use have also been declining, many observers believe that the war on drugs is gradually being won. Barry R. McCaffrey, the director of the Office of National Drug Control Policy, cites statistics showing that the overall number of illegal drug users has decreased from more than 22 million in 1979 to 12 million in 1996. The portion of the law enforcement budget targeted for combating drugs is higher than ever, as is the number of arrests for drug offenses, and there are more drug education programs in place now than ever before. In light of these developments, it would seem that the war on drugs is clearly successful.

Despite all this positive evidence, however, the many critics of the war on drugs deride the effort as a lost cause. They contend that addictive drugs such as heroin and cocaine have never been cheaper or more readily available. Moreover, they point out that the rate of teenage marijuana use doubled between 1993 and 1996. Critics also maintain that drug warriors' zeal to arrest drug offenders has resulted in an unacceptable level of prison overcrowding. Although the number of prisons nearly doubled during the Reagan and Bush administrations, prisons in many states are overflowing, largely due to increased convictions for drug offenses. Critics frequently blame these conditions not on the use of illegal drugs but on the war on drugs itself.

The viewpoints in the following chapter try to assess whether or not the war on drugs has been successful so far and whether it can be successful in the future in light of the complex problems it attempts to address.

| "Our current national drug policy is basically sound and features many successful programs."

THE WAR ON DRUGS IS SUCCEEDING

Barry R. McCaffrey

The following viewpoint is excerpted from a speech delivered to members of Congress by Barry R. McCaffrey, the director of the Office of National Drug Control Policy, commonly referred to as the "drug czar." McCaffrey contends that, far from being lost, the war on drugs has been a successful strategy that has reduced drug abuse. He objects to the "war on drugs" metaphor, preferring to depict drug abuse as a disease that must be defeated. McCaffrey suggests that the "cancer" of drug abuse must be attacked on all fronts at once, including treatment, prevention, education, enforcement, and interdiction.

As you read, consider the following questions:

1. According to McCaffrey, what critical role does law enforcement play in the war on drugs?
2. Why does McCaffrey believe that the "war" metaphor is inadequate to describe our current problem with drugs?
3. Which drug users should drug treatment programs focus on most, in the author's view?

Reprinted from Barry R. McCaffrey, "The So-Called War on Drugs: What We Must Do," address to the Senate Judiciary Committee, Washington, D.C., February 27, 1996.

We should have no doubt that illicit drug use is a major menace to public health, the safety of our society, and to the well-being of our youth.

In 1962, fewer than 4 million Americans had ever experimented with illegal drugs. Today, more than 80 million have. We are vulnerable. The good news is that most of those 80 million quit using drugs.

In the 1990s alone, illegal drug abuse has cost America more than $300 billion and 100,000 dead. At least one-third of all property crimes, assaults, or murders have a drug connection. Today, illicit drug use and tolerance of drug use by teenagers is once again rising dramatically. The damage caused to America by illegal drug use is intolerable. We must and can reduce this terrible burden on the American people.

And we can't reduce that burden without enforcement. Law enforcement is critical. Because of it, illegal cocaine costs 15 times as much as the same substance sold in legal form. Without it there would be a catastrophic rise in the availability and usage of illegal drugs.

No Silver Bullet

The metaphor "War on Drugs" is inadequate to describe this terrible menace facing the American people. Dealing with the problem of illegal drug abuse is more akin to dealing with cancer.

Wars are relatively straightforward. You identify the enemy, select a general, assign him a mission and resources, and let him get the job done. In this struggle against drug abuse, there is no silver bullet, no quick way to reduce drug use or the damage it causes.

Step number one is to mobilize the societal family—the same as when helping a cancer patient. As the President noted in the [1996] State of the Union address, "the challenge begins at home with parents talking to their children openly and firmly."

Then we must implement a long-term comprehensive plan that goes to the heart of the problem—reducing the availability of illegal drugs and their use.

It is wrong to sell drugs. This should be punished. It is also wrong to use illegal drugs. However, this is much more than a law enforcement problem. It requires a sustained and coordinated systems approach.

Clearly you can't defeat cancer if you give up hope. Nor can you make progress against illicit drug trafficking and use if you give up hope. And the answer to self-destructive proposals such as legalization is an unequivocal no.

Addressing the use and trafficking of heroin, cocaine, methamphetamine, marijuana, or other illicit drugs requires a systems approach. Each facet of the problem will require a focused program that attacks the disease while limiting damaging effects. We must design, test, and implement programs which are affordable and which do not cause unintended consequences while going after the root cause of the problem.

A LONG-TERM COMMITMENT

Addressing drug abuse requires a systems-based approach and long-term commitment.

Our current national drug policy is basically sound and features many successful programs. I have been an integral part of this strategy the past two years; we have made progress. But we need to create an operational construct that links those successes together into a coordinated effort. We also need to reach a better consensus on our strategy and to establish an active international coalition. Treatment, prevention, education, enforcement, and interdiction must all be synergistic components of that policy.

In my own view we must be even more successful in our efforts to convince American youth that experimentation with illicit drugs is dangerous. They must understand that casual drug use is like playing Russian roulette. Some of them for sure will be destroyed by addiction.

THE WAR ON DRUGS IS NOT LOST

William F. Buckley and his legalization allies proclaim that the war on drugs is lost. In fact, the two long-term scientifically conducted annual studies—the Monitoring the Future Study and the National Household Survey on Drug Abuse—reveal that since peak usage in 1979, drug use has dropped to below 13 million from 24 million among children over age 12, despite the increases of drug use among teenagers in the early 1990s.

Rachel Ehrenfeld, *Wall Street Journal*, February 7, 1996.

We must also find ways to reduce drug consumption by both adult casual and hard-core users.

However, we must focus as a priority on reducing consumption among the 3 million hard-core users who consume 75% of the total tonnage of illegal drugs. A focus of treatment programs on hard-core addicts can cause a reduction of drug-related property crimes and also drug trafficking and the violence and mayhem it spawns.

One of my early intentions will be to examine the evidence on what works and what doesn't in drug treatment programs. We owe our Congress and the American people a full accounting of the costs and payoffs of all components of our drug strategy.

Effective treatment regimes are essential to reducing drug consumption. Specifically, let me underscore my conviction that drug testing and then the treatment of convicted criminals prior to and following release from prison is vital. We simply must provide treatment to these people if we expect to protect the American people from violence and property crimes.

Finally, allow me to offer a judgment that while illicit drug use constitutes a great menace to our society the ways in which we address this challenge must be equitable and respectful of the freedoms and rights outlined by our Constitution. This is a free society and we must conduct our public policy with an absolute respect for the law.

WE ARE NOT LOSING

A lot of progress has already been made. In many ways we are not losing the so-called "War on Drugs." A decade of hard work and the support of Congress has already substantially reduced illegal drug abuse. In 1979, more than 22 million Americans used illegal drugs. Five million used cocaine. Today, less than 12 million Americans use illegal drugs regularly. Around 3 million could be classified as hard-core users, including those incarcerated. The number of cocaine users has dropped 30 percent since 1993.

But there are still serious problems to face up to.

While the number of hard-core drug users has remained steady at about 3 million, these addicts are using ever increasing tonnages of cocaine, heroin, methamphetamines, and other drugs.

Medical costs of drug abuse now exceed $20 billion per year. More than 500,000 emergency room episodes in 1995 were drug-related.

Teenage use of marijuana has doubled since 1993. This statistic tells us that our prevention programs must be more effective. We cannot cut back on these programs.

About 300 metric tons of Latin American cocaine are being smuggled into the U.S. every year along with increasing quantities of Burmese and Colombian heroin and Mexican methamphetamines.

A fundamental principle of American society is that the law must provide equal protection to all. Yet drug abuse and trafficking are having a disproportionate effect on our poor, our minorities and our cities.

We must extend a helping hand to those most in need. Many of our fellow citizens lack secure neighborhoods, safe schools, and healthy work environments. Trust in our public institutions is declining as a result. We must guarantee the safety of the families and working men and women in our urban areas.

We must reduce the harm inflicted on those sectors of our society. There can be no safe havens for drug traffickers and no tolerance for those who would employ children. We cannot tolerate open air drug markets in our cities: markets fueled by suburban money and which exacerbate the drug crisis. . . .

We will demonstrate to the American people that we can actually successfully do something about this problem. We are not helpless. We put astronauts on the moon. We beat polio and the Mafia. We won Desert Storm in 31 days and the Cold War in 45 years.

There is no reason to believe that the American people with our enormous spiritual and moral strength, our respect for law, and our compassion for our children cannot control the menace of drug abuse and the criminality it engenders.

> "The 'war on drugs' has failed to accomplish its stated objectives, and it cannot succeed so long as we remain a free society, bound by our Constitution."

THE WAR ON DRUGS IS A FAILURE

Ethan A. Nadelmann

Ethan A. Nadelmann argues in the following viewpoint that the prohibitionist approach of the war on drugs is counterproductive. He maintains that most of the problems associated with drugs are actually caused by the legal prohibition of drugs rather than drug use. The majority of drug use is victimless, according to Nadelmann, causing little harm to the user or anyone else. Since drugs cannot be eradicated from American society, Nadelmann contends, the nation's drug policy should shift its focus from prohibiting drug use to controlling the potential harm from drug abuse. A former professor of political science at Princeton University, Nadelmann is director of the Lindesmith Center, a drug-policy research institute in New York City.

As you read, consider the following questions:

1. According to Nadelmann, what medical issue is the most pervasive drug scandal in the United States?
2. What is the concept of harm reduction, as defined by the author?
3. What simple reforms need to be made right away, according to Nadelmann?

Reprinted, with permission, from Ethan A. Nadelmann, "The War on Drugs Is Lost," *National Review*, February 12, 1996; ©1996 by National Review, Inc., 215 Lexington Ave., New York, NY 10016.

The "war on drugs" has failed to accomplish its stated objectives, and it cannot succeed so long as we remain a free society, bound by our Constitution. Our prohibitionist approach to drug control is responsible for most of the ills commonly associated with America's "drug problem." And some measure of legal availability and regulation is essential if we are to reduce significantly the negative consequences of both drug use and our drug-control policies.

Proponents of the war on drugs focus on one apparent success: The substantial decline during the 1980s in the number of Americans who consumed marijuana and cocaine. Yet that decline began well before the Federal Government intensified its "war on drugs" in 1986, and it succeeded principally in reducing illicit drug use among middle-class Americans, who were least likely to develop drug-related problems.

Far more significant were the dramatic increases in drug- and prohibition-related disease, death, and crime. Crack cocaine—as much a creature of prohibition as 180-proof moonshine during alcohol prohibition—became the drug of choice in most inner cities. AIDS spread rapidly among injecting drug addicts, their lovers, and their children, while government policies restricted the availability of clean syringes that might have stemmed the epidemic. And prohibition-related violence reached unprecedented levels as a new generation of Al Capones competed for turf, killing not just one another but innocent bystanders, witnesses, and law-enforcement officials.

There are several basic truths about drugs and drug policy which a growing number of Americans have come to acknowledge.

LITTLE HARM DONE

1. Most people can use most drugs without doing much harm to themselves or anyone else. Only a tiny percentage of the 70 million Americans who have tried marijuana have gone on to have problems with that or any other drug. The same is true of the tens of millions of Americans who have used cocaine or hallucinogens. Most of those who did have a problem at one time or another don't anymore. That a few million Americans have serious problems with illicit drugs today is an issue meriting responsible national attention, but it is no reason to demonize those drugs and the people who use them.

We're unlikely to evolve toward a more effective and humane drug policy unless we begin to change the ways we think about drugs and drug control.

Perspective can be had from what is truly the most pervasive drug scandal in the United States: the epidemic of undertreatment of pain. "Addiction" to (i.e., dependence on) opiates among the terminally ill is the appropriate course of medical treatment. The only reason for the failure to prescribe adequate doses of pain-relieving opiates is the "opiaphobia" that causes doctors to ignore the medical evidence, nurses to turn away from their patients' cries of pain, and some patients themselves to elect to suffer debilitating and demoralizing pain rather than submit to a proper dose of drugs.

The tendency to put anti-drug ideology ahead of compassionate treatment of pain is apparent in another area. Thousands of Americans now smoke marijuana for purely medical reasons: among others, to ease the nausea of chemotherapy; to reduce the pain of multiple sclerosis; to alleviate the symptoms of glaucoma; to improve appetite dangerously reduced from AIDS. They use it as an effective medicine, yet they are technically regarded as criminals, and every year many are jailed. Although more than 75 per cent of Americans believe that marijuana should be available legally for medical purposes, the Federal Government refuses to legalize access or even to sponsor research.

Controlling Drug Use

2. Drugs are here to stay. The time has come to abandon the concept of a "drug-free society." We need to focus on learning to live with drugs in such a way that they do the least possible harm. So far as I can ascertain, the societies that have proved most successful in minimizing drug-related harm aren't those that have sought to banish drugs, but those that have figured out how to control and manage drug use through community discipline, including the establishment of powerful social norms. That is precisely the challenge now confronting American society regarding alcohol: How do we live with a very powerful and dangerous drug—more powerful and dangerous than many illicit drugs—that, we have learned, cannot be effectively prohibited?

Virtually all Americans have used some psychoactive substance, whether caffeine or nicotine or marijuana. In many cases, the use of cocaine and heroin represents a form of self-medication against physical and emotional pain among people who do not have access to psychotherapy or Prozac. The market in illicit drugs is as great as it is in the inner cities because palliatives for pain and depression are harder to come by and because there are fewer economic opportunities that can compete with the profits of violating prohibition.

3. Prohibition is no way to run a drug policy. We learned that with alcohol during the first third of this century and we're probably wise enough as a society not to try to repeat the mistake with nicotine. Prohibitions for kids make sense. It's reasonable to prohibit drug-related misbehavior that endangers others, such as driving under the influence of alcohol and other drugs, or smoking in enclosed spaces. But whatever its benefits in deterring some Americans from becoming drug abusers, America's indiscriminate drug prohibition is responsible for too much crime, disease, and death to qualify as sensible policy.

HARM REDUCTION STRATEGIES

4. There is a wide range of choice in drug-policy options between the free-market approach favored by Milton Friedman and Thomas Szasz, and the zero-tolerance approach of William Bennett. These options fall under the concept of harm reduction. That concept holds that drug policies need to focus on *reducing crime*, whether engendered by drugs or by the prohibition of drugs. And it holds that disease and death can be diminished even among people who can't, or won't, stop taking drugs. This pragmatic approach is followed in the Netherlands, Switzerland, Australia, and parts of Germany, Austria, Britain, and a growing number of other countries.

American drug warriors like to denigrate the Dutch, but the fact remains that Dutch drug policy has been dramatically more successful than U.S. drug policy. The average age of heroin addicts in the Netherlands has been increasing for almost a decade; HIV rates among addicts are dramatically lower than in the United States; police don't waste resources on non-disruptive drug users but, rather, focus on major dealers or petty dealers who create public nuisances. The decriminalized cannabis markets are regulated in a quasi-legal fashion far more effective and inexpensive than the U.S. equivalent.

The Swiss have embarked on a national experiment of prescribing heroin to addicts. The plan, begun in Zurich, is designed to determine whether they can reduce drug- and prohibition-related crime, disease, and death by making pharmaceutical heroin legally available to addicts at regulated clinics. The results of the experiment have been sufficiently encouraging that it is being extended to over a dozen Swiss cities. Similar experiments are being initiated by the Dutch and Australians. There are no good scientific or ethical reasons not to try a heroin-prescription experiment in the United States.

Our Federal Government puts politics over science by ignoring extensive scientific evidence that sterile syringes can reduce the spread of AIDS. Connecticut permitted needle sales in drug-stores in 1992, and the policy resulted in a 40 per cent decrease in needle sharing among injecting drug users, at no cost to tax-payers.

SOCIAL SUICIDE

Public officials must start an honest, open debate about the drug issue. Then they must let go of the self-important moralizing and the ideological posturing. The same kind of harsh, clear-eyed assessment and approach that is bringing an end to welfare-statism must be applied to the drug problem. We don't have to endorse drug use; we need only to recognize that there are more effective ways to deal with drug addiction. Our wholesale, indiscriminate prohibition policy has led to a kind of slow social suicide. It has ravaged the inner cities, decimated young blacks, corrupted the police and wasted billions of dollars on enforcement that could be spent on prevention and treatment.

Though drug warriors always use the rhetorical scare tactic of asking, "Are you going to legalize crack?," that's the wrong question to ask right now. Decriminalization can be done in steps. Recognize that whatever measures we take are not irreversible, and, as with welfare, states and cities should be encouraged to experiment until they find the best solutions. And policy-makers should enthusiastically embrace what has already been proved effective: education and prevention, treatment programs in prisons, methadone and needle exchange. They should, at the very least, do *something*. A continuation of the present policy is little more than a prescription for failure, more despair.

Craig Horowitz, *Drug Policy Letter*, Spring 1996.

We see similar foolishness when it comes to methadone. Methadone is to street heroin more or less what nicotine chewing-gum and skin patches are to cigarettes. Hundreds of studies, as well as a National Academy of Sciences report, have concluded that methadone is more effective than any other treatment in reducing heroin-related crime, disease, and death. In Australia and much of Europe, addicts who want to reduce or quit their heroin use can obtain a prescription for methadone from a GP [general practitioner] and fill the prescription at a local pharmacy. In the United States, by contrast, methadone is available only at highly regulated and expensive clinics.

A warning of the prohibitionists is that there's no going back once we reverse course and legalize drugs. But what the reforms in Europe and Australia demonstrate is that our choices are not all or nothing. Virtually all the steps described above represent modest and relatively low-risk initiatives to reduce drug- and prohibition-related harms *within our current prohibition regime*. At the same time, these steps are helpful in thinking through the consequences of more far-reaching drug-policy reform. You don't need to go for formal legalization to embark on numerous reforms that would yield great dividends. But these run into opiaphobia.

The blame is widespread. Cowardly presidents, unwilling to assume leadership for reform. A Congress so concerned with appearing tough on crime that it is unwilling to analyze alternative approaches. A drug czar who debases public debate by equating legalization with genocide. A drug enforcement/treatment complex so hooked on government dollars that the antidrug crusade has become a vested interest.

But perhaps the worst offender is the U.S. Drug Enforcement Administration—not so much the agents who risk their lives trying to apprehend major drug traffickers as the ideologically driven bureaucrats who intimidate and persecute doctors for prescribing pain medication in medically appropriate (but legally suspicious) doses, who hobble methadone programs with their overregulation, who acknowledge that law enforcement alone cannot solve the drug problem but then proceed to undermine innovative public-health initiatives.

RESISTANCE TO REFORM

I am often baffled by the resistance of conservatives to drug-policy reform, but encouraged by the willingness of many to reassess their views once they have heard the evidence. Conservatives who oppose the expansion of federal power cannot look approvingly on the growth of the federal drug-enforcement bureaucracy and federal efforts to coerce states into adopting federally formulated drug policies. Those who focus on the victimization of Americans by predatory criminals can hardly support our massive diversion of law-enforcement resources to apprehending and imprisoning nonviolent vice merchants and consumers. Those concerned with overregulation can hardly countenance our current handling of methadone, our refusal to allow over-the-counter sale of sterile syringes, our prohibition of medical marijuana. And conservatives who turn to the Bible for guidance on current affairs can find little justification there for our war on drugs and the people who use and sell them.

| "Strong drug enforcement in the United States is correlated with reductions in crime, drug use, and drug addiction growth rates."

LAW ENFORCEMENT IS WINNING THE WAR ON DRUGS

Robert E. Peterson

In the following viewpoint, Robert E. Peterson disputes the common assertion that the war on drugs is too punitive and is failing. He cites crime statistics from the past forty years to support his argument that drug enforcement measures have not been excessively harsh and that high rates of incarceration in recent years have led to declining rates of crime, teen drug use, and drug arrests. Peterson, former director of the Michigan Office of Drug Control Policy, is a lawyer in private practice in Owego, New York.

As you read, consider the following questions:

1. According to the author, why is the difference between arrest rates and incarceration rates for drug offenses significant?
2. In the author's view, what years constituted the era of permissiveness in drug enforcement?
3. In 1979, what percentage of high school students smoked marijuana every day of the week, according to Peterson?

Reprinted from the Overview, pages 1–6, of Robert E. Peterson, Drug Enforcement Works! (Vestal, NY: O'Grady Press, 1997), by permission of the author. Copyright 1997 by Robert E. Peterson.

Strong drug enforcement in the United States is correlated with reductions in crime, drug use, and drug addiction growth rates. The positive impact of tougher drug sanctions has been overshadowed by a prevalent myth that U.S. drug enforcement has become "too punitive" or is a failed approach that should be replaced with a "public health" strategy by diverting enforcement resources into treatment programs.

This myth has been packaged and promoted by the multi-million-dollar pro–drug legalization lobby, civil libertarians, and misguided academic researchers to the media and public with limited critical review and challenge. The evidence and studies purporting to demonstrate that the "drug war has failed" are themselves failed studies that distort facts to make an ideological argument.

Over $20 million has recently been put into efforts to discredit law enforcement as an approach to drug problems and to promote various schemes of drug legalization and decriminalization. A single donor committed $15 million to several such organizations, led by top legalization advocates.

EFFECTIVE AND EFFICIENT

There is strong objective evidence that strong drug law enforcement has a positive impact in curtailing drug related crime and drug use. Historical experience warns that weakening drug enforcement leads to increased societal costs and problems.

Over the past decade the criminal justice system improved its effectiveness and efficiency responding to serious drug crimes, especially against cocaine and heroin traffickers. Law enforcement is an effective strategy to reduce crime and drug related problems and costs and crime has dropped for five straight years [1991–1996]. . . .

Those critical of drug enforcement often create a false dichotomy by forcing a choice between law enforcement or treatment and prevention. The truth is that U.S. drug policy has never excluded one for the other. Law enforcement complements treatment and prevention efforts and national drug policy has always included public health approaches. This viewpoint does not argue that only an enforcement approach is needed, or that enforcement alone brought about successes.

Attacks on drug enforcement efforts often hold law enforcement to impossible and changing performance standards. None of the credit for a dramatic twelve-year decline in drug use among our children is attributed to law enforcement, yet recent increases in drug use are cited as evidence of enforcement's failure. A rise in any type of crime is more "evidence" of enforcement's failure; sustained drops in crime victimization and recently of crime rates overall are not properly correlated with tough drug enforcement.

This viewpoint does not propose that drug enforcement has, can, or will solve all of society's drug and crime problems. It does demonstrate that tough drug enforcement is correlated with many positive benefits and indicates that permissive drug policies are correlated with increased social problems and costs. . . .

PERMISSIVE DRUG POLICIES

The prevailing myth is that the U.S. has taken a progressively tougher drug enforcement stance for the past 30 years and that this "punitive" approach has not been successful or beneficial.

Drug enforcement critics often correlate raw drug arrest or imprisonment numbers with isolated crime, drug use, or other statistics. Drug statutes also have been taken out of context to demonstrate the supposed "harshness" of drug laws. Public perceptions that drug problems are growing worse supplant objective data on the topic.

There are two fundamental errors in this approach. First, drug enforcement and laws never did get progressively "tougher" over the past three decades. Drug permissiveness reigned for the first two decades.

Second, many of the most crucial measures of the dependent variable, the "drug problem," are ignored and have dramatically improved over time. These successes are conveniently ignored.

The basic premise that the U.S. undertook an increasingly punitive criminal justice approach to drugs since the 1960's is inaccurate and based on faulty measures. It relies on raw arrest numbers. A more "punitive" drug policy would bring about greater consequences and punishment to those arrested, not just increase arrests.

When "toughness" or "punitive" is redefined from arrest and incarceration numbers to measuring the proportion of drug arrestees actually incarcerated, one finds that the nation entered a period of drug permissiveness beginning in 1960 and ending in 1980.

The drug incarceration rate plummeted 79% from 1960–1980, as drug laws were weakened and decriminalization of some drugs was experimented with. It was not until 1990 that the drug incarceration rate rose to the level it was at in 1960.

In the late 1970's, drug tolerance and leniency reached a peak in the U.S. Federal drug information downplayed the health hazards of marijuana and cocaine, and in 1974, the man later appointed President Carter's drug czar wrote that cocaine was "benign." In 1977, the nation's drug czar was reported to have snorted cocaine at the national marijuana smokers lobby's Christmas party.

The President's drug advisor called for marijuana decriminalization and review of whether cocaine should be illegal. A dozen states decriminalized marijuana and the drug paraphernalia business was a multi-million-dollar industry.

LAW ENFORCEMENT REDUCES DRUG USE

In point of fact, as enforcement increased in the 1980s there were dramatic declines in *overall* drug use. There is at least some evidence, then, as reflected in use and health care statistics, to suggest that law enforcement can reduce drug use and addiction rates. There is no evidence to suggest that ending drug law enforcement efforts will lower use rates or the harm done by addiction. In fact, evidence indicates that it is law enforcement and criminal justice pressure that leads many addicts into treatment who would otherwise not seek help.

Still, advocates of a serious enforcement policy never claim that it would end drug use. The aim is to protect the public from the worst predators, engage in a struggle to reverse the trend of increasing drug use throughout the population, and send an unambiguous signal to potential new users that drug use has negative social consequences.

William J. Olson, *Heritage Foundation Backgrounder*, July 18, 1994.

Drug arrests were made, but consequences were rare. Drug incarceration rates reached a historical low point. Only 20 of every 1,000 drug criminals were incarcerated from 1975–1980. Drugs were glamorized through movies, music, and pop culture.

Drug education gave glowing accounts of drug effects, demonstrations of drug use, and minimization of drug harms. So-called "harm reduction" tactics taught children the "responsible use" of drugs.

Not surprisingly, drug use among children skyrocketed, reaching a high point in 1979, when one in ten high school seniors was stoned on marijuana every day of the week. Cocaine and hallucinogen use also reached record levels. No civilized nation has ever had so many young teens using mind-altering chemicals.

With drug enforcement consequences low, crime was rampant—violence rose 82% over the decade. There were 5.3 million more crimes at the end of the decade and a record murder rate. States that decriminalized marijuana increased hospital emergency admissions for pot and youth drug use.

The drug incarceration rate bottomed out in 1980, the year that murder rates reached a peak high point and drug use was at near record levels.

THE IMPACT OF TOUGH DRUG LAWS

It is during a period of drug permissiveness and weak punitive sanctions that a dramatic rise in crime and violence swept across America.

The decline in drug offender incarceration rates was steep and sudden. In 1960, for every 1,000 drug arrests, 90 drug offenders were incarcerated. By 1980 that figure reached a low point of only 19 of every 1,000 offenders being incarcerated. The peak year for murder and other serious crimes also was in 1980, when drug incarcerations were at an all-time low and drug use was at an all-time high.

The dramatic rise in drug use among children and adults and explosion of violence experienced during the past three decades in the U.S. transpired when drug incarceration rates fell below 1960 levels.

The peak years for murder and violent and property crime in the U.S. were 1978–1980, when drug incarceration rates reached their lowest ebb. After 1980, crime rates began to stabilize and have declined as drug incarceration rates increased. The crime rate began falling again in 1991, as drug incarceration rates reached record levels. For five straight years serious crime rates have been dropping, a 12% decline from 1991–1996 (est). Burglary rates hit a twenty-five-year low point in 1995 and murders fell 14% from 1991–1996. New York City experienced annual homicide drops.

Falling Drug Incarceration
As drug incarceration rates fell 79% from 1960–1980:
• Drug use among teens climbed more than 500%
• Drug addiction rates rose, with heroin use climbing 900%
• Violent crime increased 270%, on average up 13% per year
• Property crime increased 210%
• Burglary increased 230%
• Murders increased 100%
• Robberies increased 318%

Rising Drug Incarceration
As drug incarceration rates rose 447% from 1980–1995:
• Murder rate declined 21% (est 27% 1980–1996)

- Robberies declined 10%
- Burglary declined 41% (est 44% 1980–1996)
- Serious crimes declined 11% (est 14% 1980–1996)
- Property crime declined 13% (est 14% 1980–1996)
- High school drug use declined by more than a third
- Violent crime rate growth slowed from +13% to 1% per year (and was lower in 1996 than in 1989)
- Heavy cocaine use fell 11% and heavy heroin use 17% from 1988

The U.S. drug budget was primarily weighted toward treatment until the mid-1970's. This policy was accompanied with a great increase in youth drug use and a rise in heroin addiction rates.

Historical experience indicates that only arresting drug offenders is not effective—offenders must face consequences and risk incarceration to have an impact. When the U.S. abandoned a permissive addict-dominated drug policy, the growth in drug use and crime was abated.

| "Sadly, the police have been pushed into a war they did not start and cannot win."

LAW ENFORCEMENT CANNOT WIN THE WAR ON DRUGS

Joseph D. McNamara

According to Joseph D. McNamara, a growing percentage of police chiefs in the United States believe that the war on drugs cannot be won by the current law enforcement approach to the problem. McNamara contends that because the profit margin for selling drugs is so high, there will always be people willing to take the risk. McNamara, who has been the chief of police in several large cities, is a research fellow of the Hoover Institution in Stanford, California, and has written four books on policing.

As you read, consider the following questions:

1. What does McNamara mean by the term "vested interests" in describing the resistance to changing the drug laws?
2. According to McNamara, why do police so often get drawn into drug scandals?
3. What do the majority of police chiefs favor over more arrests and prisons for drug offenders?

Reprinted, with permission, from Joseph D. McNamara, "The War on Drugs Is Lost," *National Review*, February 12, 1996; ©1996 by National Review, Inc., 215 Lexington Ave., New York, NY 10016.

"It's the money, stupid." After 35 years as a police officer in three of the country's largest cities, that is my message to the righteous politicians who obstinately proclaim that a war on drugs will lead to a drug-free America. About $500 worth of heroin or cocaine in a source country will bring in as much as $100,000 on the streets of an American city. All the cops, armies, prisons, and executions in the world cannot impede a market with that kind of tax-free profit margin. It is the illegality that permits the obscene markup, enriching drug traffickers, distributors, dealers, crooked cops, lawyers, judges, politicians, bankers, businessmen.

Vested Interests

Naturally, these people are against reform of the drug laws. Drug crooks align themselves with their avowed enemies, such as the Drug Enforcement Administration, in opposing drug reform. They are joined by many others with vested economic interests. President Eisenhower warned of a military-industrial complex that would elevate the defense budget unnecessarily. That military-industrial complex pales in comparison to the host of industries catering to our national puritanical hypocrisy— researchers willing to tell the government what it wants to hear, prison builders, correction and parole officers' associations, drug-testing companies, and dubious purveyors of anti-drug education. . . .

Sadly, the police have been pushed into a war they did not start and cannot win. It was not the police who lobbied in 1914 for passage of the Harrison Act, which first criminalized drugs. It was the Protestant missionary societies in China, the Woman's Christian Temperance Union, and other such organizations that viewed the taking of psychoactive substances as sinful. These groups gradually got their religious tenets enacted into penal statutes under which the "sinners" go to jail. The religious origin is significant for two reasons. If drugs had been outlawed because the police had complained that drug use caused crime and disorder, the policy would have been more acceptable to the public and won more compliance. And the conviction that the use of certain drugs is immoral chills the ability to scrutinize rationally and to debate the effects of the drug war. When Ethan Nadelmann pointed out once that it was illogical for the most hazardous drugs, alcohol and nicotine, to be legal while less dangerous drugs were illegal, he was roundly denounced. A leading conservative supporter of the drug war contended that while alcohol and nicotine addiction was unhealthy and could even cost lives, addiction to illegal drugs could result in the loss of one's soul. No empirical proof was given.

Anti-Drug Rhetoric

The demonizing of these drugs and their users encourages demagoguery. William Bennett, the nation's first drug czar, would cut off the heads of drug sellers. Bennett's anti-drug rhetoric is echoed by Joseph Califano, the liberal former Secretary of Health, Education, and Welfare, now chairman of the Center on Addiction and Substance Abuse at Columbia University. In June 1995, the Center hysterically suggested (with great media coverage) that binge drinking and other substance abuse were taking over the nation's colleges, leading to an increase in rapes, assaults, and murders and to the spread of AIDS and other sexually transmitted diseases. The validity of the research in Califano's report was persuasively debunked by Kathy McNamara-Meis, writing in Forbes Media Critic. She was equally critical of the media for accepting the Center's sensational statements.

Conservatives like Bennett normally advocate minimal government. Liberals like Califano ordinarily recoil from the draconian prison sentences and property seizures used in the drug war. This illustrates why it is so difficult to get politicians to concede that alternative approaches to drug control need to be studied. We are familiar with the perception that the first casualty in any war is truth. Eighty years of drug-war propaganda have so influenced public opinion that most politicians believe they will lose their jobs if their opponents can claim they are soft on drugs and crime. Yet, public doubt is growing. Gallup reports that in 1990 only 4 per cent of Americans believed that "arresting the people who use drugs" is the best way for the government to allocate resources.

Personal Experience

It was my own experience as a policeman trying to enforce the laws against drugs that led me to change my attitude about drug-control policy. The analogy to the Vietnam War is fitting. I was a willing foot soldier at the start of the modern drug war, pounding a beat in Harlem. During the early 1960s, as heroin use spread, we made many arrests, but it did not take long before cops realized that arrests did not lessen drug selling or drug use.

I came to realize just how ineffective we were in deterring drug use one day when my partner and I arrested an addict for possession of a hypodermic needle and heroin. Our prisoner had already shot up, but the heroin charge we were prepared to level at him was based on the tiny residue in the bottle cap used to heat the fix. It was petty, but then—and now—such arrests are valued because they can be used to claim success, like the body counts during the Vietnam War.

In this case the addict offered to "give" us a pusher in exchange for letting him go. He would lure the pusher into a hallway where we could then arrest him in the act of selling drugs. We trailed the addict along Lenox Avenue. To our surprise, he spoke to one man after another.

It suddenly struck me as humiliating, the whole scene. Here it was, broad daylight. We were brilliantly visible, in uniform, in a marked police car: and yet a few feet away, our quarry was attempting one drug transaction after another. The first two dealers weren't deterred by our presence—they were simply sold out, and we could not arrest them without the goods. We finally arrested the third pusher, letting the first addict escape, as we had covenanted. The man we brought in was selling drugs only to support his own habit.

QUESTIONABLE BEHAVIOR

Another inherent difficulty in drug enforcement is that violators are engaging in consensual activity and seek privacy. Every day, millions of drug crimes similar to what took place in front of our police car occur without police knowledge. To enforce drug laws the police have to resort to undercover work, which is dangerous to them and also to innocent bystanders. Drug enforcement often involves questionable ethical behavior by the police, such as what we did in letting a guilty person go free because he enticed someone else into violating the law.

Soldiers in a war need to dehumanize the enemy, and many cops look on drug users as less than human. The former police chief of Los Angeles, Daryl Gates, testified before the United States Senate that casual users should be taken out and shot. He defended the statement to the *Los Angeles Times* by saying, "We're in a war." New York police officers convicted of beating and robbing drug dealers (their boss at the time became Director of the White House's Office of National Drug Control Policy) rationalized their crimes by saying it was impossible to stop drug dealing and these guys were the enemy. Why should they get to keep all the money?

Police scandals are an untallied cost of the drug war. The FBI, the Drug Enforcement Administration, and even the Coast Guard have had to admit to corruption. The gravity of the police crimes is as disturbing as the volume. In New Orleans, a uniformed cop in league with a drug dealer has been convicted of murdering her partner and shop owners during a robbery committed while she was on patrol. In Washington, D.C., and in Atlanta, cops in drug stings were arrested for stealing and taking bribes. New York State troopers falsified drug evidence that sent people to prison.

And it is not just the rank and file. The former police chief of Detroit went to prison for stealing police drug-buy money. In a small New England town, the chief stole drugs from the evidence locker for his own use. And the DEA agent who arrested Panama's General Noriega is in jail for stealing laundered drug money.

Gary Markstein. Reprinted by permission of Copley News Service.

The drug war is as lethal as it is corrupting. And the police and drug criminals are not the only casualties. An innocent 75-year-old African-American minister died of a heart attack struggling with Boston cops who were mistakenly arresting him because an informant had given them the wrong address. A rancher in Ventura County, California, was killed by a police SWAT team serving a search warrant in the mistaken belief that he was growing marijuana. In Los Angeles, a three-year-old girl died of gunshot wounds after her mother took a wrong turn into a street controlled by a drug-dealing gang. They fired on the car because it had invaded their marketplace.

The violence comes from the competition for illegal profits among dealers, not from crazed drug users. Professor Milton Friedman has estimated that as many as 10,000 additional homicides a year are plausibly attributed to the drug war.

Worse still, the drug war has become a race war in which non-whites are arrested and imprisoned at 4 to 5 times the rate whites are, even though most drug crimes are committed by whites. The Sentencing Research Project reports that one-third of black men are in jail or under penal supervision, largely because of drug arrests. The drug war has established thriving criminal enterprises which recruit teenagers into criminal careers.

POLICE CHIEFS VOTE NO CONFIDENCE

It was such issues that engaged law-enforcement leaders—most of them police chiefs—from fifty agencies during a two-day conference at the Hoover Institution in May 1995. Among the speakers was Baltimore Mayor Kurt Schmoke, who told the group that he had visited a high school and asked the students if the high dropout rate was due to kids' being hooked on drugs. He was told that the kids were dropping out because they were hooked on drug money, not drugs. He also told us that when he went to community meetings he would ask the audience three questions. 1) "Have we won the drug war?" People laughed. 2) "Are we winning the drug war?" People shook their heads. 3) "If we keep doing what we are doing will we have won the drug war in ten years?" The answer was a resounding No.

At the end of the conference, the police participants completed an evaluation form. Ninety per cent voted no confidence in the war on drugs. They were unanimous in favoring more treatment and education over more arrests and prisons. They were unanimous in recommending a presidential blue-ribbon commission to evaluate the drug war and to explore alternative methods of drug control. In sum, the tough-minded law-enforcement officials took positions directly contrary to those of Congress and the President.

One hopes that politicians will realize that no one can accuse them of being soft on drugs if they vote for changes suggested by many thoughtful people in law enforcement. If the politicians tone down their rhetoric it will permit police leaders to expose the costs of our present drug-control policies. Public opinion will then allow policy changes to decriminalize marijuana and stop the arrest of hundreds of thousands of people every year. The enormous savings can be used for what the public really wants—the prevention of violent crime.

| "We can reduce drug use without compromising American ideals if we maintain adequate resolve."

THE PROHIBITION STRATEGY CAN WIN THE WAR ON DRUGS

Office of National Drug Control Policy

Each year, the Office of National Drug Control Policy issues its *National Drug Control Strategy*. In the following viewpoint, an excerpt from the 1997 edition of this publication, the ONDCP contends that while much remains to be done, the overall strategy of prohibition in the war on drugs is a necessary and a largely successful approach. The authors point to the dramatic decline in the overall number of drug users during the past twenty years as evidence of the policy's effectiveness. However, noting an increase in teenage drug use in recent years, the authors call for a renewed moral resolve and a commitment to the prohibition message that declares intolerance for drug use in the United States.

As you read, consider the following questions:

1. In the view of the authors, at what time intervals does the public express alarm over the dangers of drug use?
2. Why is the term "war on drugs" a misleading metaphor, as explained by the authors?
3. According to the authors, what percentage of all Americans aged twelve and older have tried an illicit drug?

Reprinted from *The National Drug Control Strategy*, 1997, a publication of the Office of Drug Control Policy, February 1997.

The first duty of government is to protect its citizens. The Constitution of the United States—as interpreted over 208 years—articulates the obligation of the federal government to uphold the public good, providing a bulwark against all threats, foreign and domestic. Illegal drugs constitute one such threat. Toxic, addictive substances present a hazard to society as a whole. Like a corrosive, insidious cancer, drug abuse diminishes the potential of our citizens for full growth and development.

The traditions of American government and democracy affirm self-determination and freedom. While government must minimize interference in the private lives of citizens, it cannot deny security to individuals and the collective culture the people uphold. Drug abuse and its consequences destroy personal liberty and the well-being of communities. Crime, violence, antisocial behavior, accidents, unintended pregnancies, drug-exposed infants, and addiction are only part of the price illegal drug use imposes on society. Every drug user risks his ability to think rationally and his potential for a full, productive life. Drug abuse drains the physical and moral strength of America. It spawns global criminal syndicates and bankrolls those who sell drugs to children. Illegal drugs foster crime and violence in our inner cities, suburbs, and rural areas.

THE EBB AND FLOW OF DRUG USE

Drug-induced deaths increased 47 percent between 1990 and 1994 and number approximately 14,000 a year. Illegal drugs also burden our society with approximately $67 billion in social, health, and criminal costs each year. Absent effective government action, the damage to our country would be even greater. Historians have documented America's experience with addictive drugs over the past two hundred years. The ebb and flow of drug use recurred in roughly thirty-year cycles: an uninformed or forgetful public becomes indifferent to the dangers of rising drug use only to recoil at its devastating consequences. For the benefit of all Americans, the 1997 *National Drug Control Strategy* sets a steady course to reduce drug abuse and its detrimental consequences. . . .

A BALANCED PROGRAM IS NEEDED

Reducing the drug problem in America requires a multi-faceted, balanced program. We cannot hope to decrease drug abuse by relying exclusively on one approach. William Bennett laid out in the 1989 *National Drug Control Strategy* a lesson that still applies today: ". . . no single tactic—pursued alone or to the detriment of other possible and valuable initiatives—can work to contain or reduce drug use." We can expect no panacea, no "silver bullet." We can neither arrest nor educate our way out of this problem. The 1997 *Strategy* presents a range of approaches that promise, when taken together, to decrease illegal drug use in America. . . .

Some people believe that drug use is so deeply embedded in society that we can never hope to decrease it. Others feel that the problem can be solved in short order if draconian measures are adopted. Avoiding extremes, the *Strategy* rejects both of these views. We can reduce drug use without compromising American ideals if we maintain adequate resolve. . . .

AN ENDURING CHALLENGE

Drug abuse has plagued America for more than a century. To turn that negative experience around will require perseverance and vigilance. Our nation can contain and decrease the damage wrought by drug abuse and its consequences. But we will have to apply ourselves with a resolve marked by continuing education for our citizens, the determination to resist criminals who traffic in illegal drugs, and the patience and compassion to treat individuals caught in the grip of illegal drugs.

The metaphor of a "war on drugs" is misleading. Wars are expected to end. Addressing drug abuse is a continuous challenge; the moment we believe ourselves to be victorious and free to relax our resolve, drug abuse will rise again. Furthermore, the United States does not wage war on its citizens, many of whom are the victims of drug abuse. These individuals must be helped, not defeated. It is the suppliers of illegal drugs, both foreign and domestic, who must be thwarted. . . .

FEWER AMERICANS ARE USING ILLEGAL DRUGS

An estimated 12.8 million Americans, about 6 percent of the household population aged twelve and older, use illegal drugs on a current basis (within the past thirty days). This number of "past-month" drug users has declined by almost 50 percent from the 1979 high of twenty-five million—a decrease that represents an extraordinary change in behavior. Despite the dramatic drop, more than a third of all Americans twelve and older have tried an illicit drug. Ninety percent of those who have used illegal drugs used marijuana or hashish. Approximately a third used cocaine or took a prescription type drug for nonmedical reasons. About a fifth used LSD. Fortunately, nearly sixty million Americans who used illicit drugs during youth, as adults reject these substances.

Many Americans believe that drug abuse is not their problem. They have misconceptions that drug users belong to a segment of society different from their own or that drug abuse is remote from their environment. They are wrong. Almost three quarters of drug users are employed. A majority of Americans believe that drug use and drug-related crime are among our nation's most pressing social problems. Approximately 45 percent of Americans know someone with a substance abuse problem.

Past-Month Users of any Illicit Drugs, Marijuana, and Cocaine

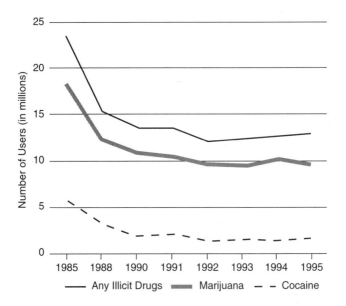

Source: National Household Survey on Drug Abuse, National Institute on Drug Abuse (1985-91), Substance Abuse and Mental Health Services Administration, (1992-95)

While drug use and its consequences threaten Americans of every socio-economic background, geographic region, educational level, and ethnic and racial identity, the effects of drug use are often felt disproportionally. Neighborhoods where illegal drug markets flourish are plagued by attendant crime and violence. Americans who lack comprehensive health plans and have smaller incomes may be less able to afford treatment programs to overcome drug dependence. What all Americans must understand is that no one is immune from the consequences of drug use. Every family is vulnerable. We must make a commitment to reducing drug abuse and not mistakenly assume that illegal drugs are someone else's concern. . . .

MORE WORK REMAINS

We have made progress in our efforts to reduce drug use and its consequences in America. While America's illegal drug problem is serious, it does not approach the emergency situation of the late 1970s or the cocaine epidemic in the 1980s. Just 6 percent of our household population age twelve and over was using drugs in 1995, down from 14.1 percent in 1979. Fewer than 1 percent were using cocaine, inhalants, or hallucinogens. The most-commonly-used illegal drug was marijuana, taken by 77 percent of drug users.

As drug use became less prevalent through the 1980s, national attention to the drug problem decreased. The Partnership for a Drug-Free America suggests that an indicator or that decreased attention was the reduced frequency of anti-drug public service announcements (PSAs) on TV, radio, and in print media. Our children also dropped their guard as drugs became less prevalent and first-hand knowledge of dangerous substances became scarce. Consequently, disapproval of drugs and the perception of risk on the part of young people has declined throughout this decade. As a result, since 1992 more youth have been using alcohol, tobacco, and illegal drugs.

A disturbing study prepared by CASA [Columbia University's Center on Addiction and Substance Abuse] suggests that adults have become resigned to teen drug use. In fact, nearly half the parents from the "baby-boomer" generation expect their teenagers to try illegal drugs. Forty percent believe they have little influence over teenagers' decisions about whether to smoke, drink, or use illegal drugs. Both of these assumptions are incorrect. Parents have enormous influence over the decisions young people make.

REVERSING NEGATIVE TRENDS

The United States has failed to forestall resurgent drug use among children in the '90s. This problem did not develop recently. The 1993 *Interim National Drug Control Strategy* highlighted the problem of rising drug use among American youth, quoting the 1992 *Monitoring the Future* study which found that eighth graders and college students were ". . . reporting higher rates of drug use in 1992 than they did in 1991. Further, fewer eighth graders in 1992 perceived great risk with using cocaine or crack than did eighth graders in 1991." The continuation of these trends has been substantiated by every significant survey of drug use since 1993.

Our challenge is to reverse these negative trends. America cannot allow the relapse we have experienced to signal a return to catastrophic illegal drug use levels of the past. The government has committed itself to that end; so have nongovernmental organizations. . . . Working together, we can succeed.

| "Continuing legal prohibition *as the* major strategy for combating drugs is to attempt the impossible, by means that have already been discredited."

PROHIBITION IS A LOSING STRATEGY IN THE WAR ON DRUGS

Dwight B. Heath

In contrast to those who argue that the prohibition of drugs is winning the war on drugs, Dwight B. Heath points to the negative effects of this strategy in the United States. Contrasting American drug policy with some European alternatives to prohibition, he suggests that many facets of the "drug problem" in America derive from the war on drugs itself. For example, according to Heath, increased incarceration results in racial imbalances in prosecution, in broken families, and in the overcrowding of both courts and prisons. Heath is a professor of anthropology at Brown University.

As you read, consider the following questions:

1. According to Heath, how did the public respond to President Bush's call for a "war on drugs" in 1989?
2. How has massive incarceration of drug offenders in recent years affected the overall crime rate, according to the author?
3. In Heath's view, what can be learned from study of the Dutch system of drug laws?

Reprinted from Dwight B. Heath, "The War on Drugs as a Metaphor in American Culture," in *Drug Policy and Human Nature*, edited by Warren K. Bickel and Richard J. DeGrandpre (New York: Plenum Press, 1996), by permission of the author and publisher.

George Bush had been President of the United States for half a year, elected by a landslide victory and inaugurated in a time of welling chauvinism and superficial prosperity. The American people seemed eager to hear his plans when he gave his first televised address in August of 1989. Whatever disappointment there may have been over pressing needs that were not mentioned, his call to arms in the war on drugs struck a responsive chord. During the next several months, the media was full of feature stories, editorials, news reports, and background accounts about "the drug menace," the "war on drugs," and a host of other approaches to drug use and its deadly impact. At one level the imagery of war could be viewed as just a metaphor, a rhetorical device virtually guaranteed to galvanize public opinion, demonstrate the speaker's decisiveness, rally support, and draw a sharp line between "us" and "them." No longer a wimp, as he had earlier been characterized, Pres. Bush had identified a common enemy, announced a firm stand, and promised to take action to "defeat" the other side. Such rhetoric on the part of other presidents had been applauded in connection with the "war on poverty" and the "war on illiteracy," as it had been earlier with the "war against drink" and, probably, in a series of other pseudoevents in American history. . . .

Within a month of Pres. Bush's call to arms, public opinion polls reported that nearly 65% of the American people were identifying drugs as "the major issue facing this country," and there appeared to be remarkable consensus in support of a militant agenda against them. . . .

CONTINUING FAILURE IN THE WAR ON DRUGS

Despite the flurry of concern that followed Pres. Bush's call to arms [in 1989], media and popular concern flagged early as economic recession worsened, and there was recognition that the highly touted policies were winning few battles and held no promise of winning the war; similar lack of media coverage continues under Pres. Clinton. The General Accounting Office (GAO) and various Congressional committees issued authoritative reports that contradicted assertions of the National Office of Drug Control Policy and revealed major methodological and arithmetic flaws in the Office's calculations. People became aware that interdiction could not be effective and that there was not even support for treatment of those addicts who requested it. Ever larger quantities of drugs, at even lower prices, told the lie to a supply side approach. Although few U.S. citizens were aware of it, growing resentment of U.S. drug-related intervention abroad was eroding the patience of some of our allies.

Another aspect of the war on drugs that some prefer to ignore, and others would eagerly change, is the mushrooming rate of prison construction and incarceration. With 455 per 100,000 of the population in jails or prisons, the United States now has the dubious distinction of leading the world—far ahead of South Africa, second with 311. By way of contrast, Japan's rate is only 34. While Pres. Bush's Attorney General rated this a sign of success and called for more prison space as the only alternative to more crime, a growing number of critics now view with dismay the expansion that has already occurred and consider it a monument to society's failure in terms of economic opportunities, racial discrimination, education, and other respects.

INCARCERATION AND THE CRIME RATE

Although the rhetoric of the "war on drugs" has cooled somewhat and domestic economic and political issues have come to the fore in terms of journalistic attention during Clinton's presidency, there has been little change in governmental policy or police and military actions. More than half of the prison population are still there on drug charges, with blacks and Hispanics disproportionately represented. According to government statistics . . . , federal and state prison populations have increased by 90% since the mid-1980s, while the crime rate (adjusted for population) remains virtually unchanged. It is evident that massive incarceration has had little effect in reducing crime. Increased reliance on mandatory sentencing, eliminating parole, and building more jail cells has nothing to do with rehabilitation and apparently accomplishes little in the way of deterrence. Poverty, broken families, and unacculturated immigrants are often cited as important causal factors, but the experience of other countries and the historical precedent in the United States both suggest that other, more fundamental, factors must be involved.

Every major city has had too many incidents in which an innocent bystander was shot, but the majority of drug-related violence is directed against competing drug dealers. In similar fashion, although many addicts resort to theft and a variety of petty deceptive schemes to support their habit, those most frequently victimized by such "hustles" are their friends, family, and acquaintances rather than wealthier strangers.

DISCRIMINATION IN DRUG LAW ENFORCEMENT

Selective detention may be part of the problem, with a persistent pattern of racial and ethnic prejudice acted out daily, as police harass innocent members of one group and are overly tolerant of another. This is not a universal pattern, but it occurs far too often. Similarly, repeated studies have shown that, although justice can't be bought in a simple straightforward transaction, minority suspects with lower income and education are disproportionately booked by police. In 1989, with blacks comprising 12% of the population, 42% of drug arrests were of blacks. In the same way, among defendants who are tried, those of minority status with lower income and education are disproportionately sentenced, and their sentences are consistently, and significantly, more severe, even for similar offenses. To call such discrimination genocidal is polemical overstatement, but to call it normal would be a terrible indictment of our legal system.

MORE HARM THAN GOOD

I believe that a drug-free America is a utopian dream. Some form of drug addiction or substance abuse is endemic in most societies. Insisting on the total eradication of drug use can only lead to failure and disappointment. The war on drugs cannot be won; but, like the Vietnam War, it has polarized our society.

And its adverse effects over time may be even more devastating. Criminalizing drug abuse does more harm than good, blocking effective treatment and incarcerating far too many people. Our prison and jail population—now more than a million and a half—has doubled over the past decade and more than tripled since 1980. The number of drug law violators behind bars has increased eightfold since 1980, to about 400,000 people. . . .

Unfortunately the present climate is inimical to a well-balanced drug policy. Crusading advocates of prohibition and deterrence—Rosenthal, Califano, McCaffrey and others—stand in the way of reasoned discussion. They insist that there is only one solution to the drug problem, namely, the "war on drugs" and that those who are critical of present policies are enemies of society. Few elected officials dare to incur their wrath. Hysteria has replaced debate in the public discourse.

George Soros, *Washington Post National Weekly Edition*, February 10, 1997.

In a sense, even those who are not members of the discriminated minorities are being hurt by the heavy involvement that the criminal justice system has in prosecuting the war on drugs. In many jurisdictions the police are so burdened with drug issues that other aspects of their work are often neglected. Courts are incredibly overcrowded, as are jails and prisons. Associated costs add a significant burden to already strained budgets, resulting in escalating taxes that weigh heavily on already over-taxed constituents.

An inner-city individual's occasional "success" (in wealth, prestige, and so forth) associated with drugs is taken by many as evidence that "the system" is failing and that amoral behavior is rewarded. However rare they may be, instances of corruption among police, judges, and other government agents carry the same message. Rightly or wrongly, drugs are associated with the high drop-out rate in schools, slow learning, teenage pregnancy, accelerating unemployment, falling productivity, the cost of social welfare, and a host of other aspects of contemporary life that people find annoying and discouraging.

Ironically, some of the problems that can be directly and unequivocally linked with excessive use of drugs—such as the costs of rehabilitation and treatment, and the maintenance of impaired infants—are even more significant than seems to be recognized by many who complain most loudly about drugs and their negative impact on society. . . .

PROHIBITION POLICIES HARM SOCIETY

What is being ignored in the dominant image of "the drug problem" in the United States today is the fact that so many of the ills that are cited derive more from the prohibition policies that are in effect than from the use of drugs as such. Ethan A. Nadelmann succinctly phrased it: "The greatest beneficiaries of the drug laws are organized and unorganized drug traffickers. The criminalization of the drug market effectively imposes a de facto value-added tax that is enforced and occasionally augmented by the law enforcement establishment and collected by the drug traffickers." The same occurred earlier with the prohibition of alcohol in the United States and more recently with strict controls on the availability of alcohol in the former Soviet Union.

The presumed connections among drugs, crime, violence, and disturbed youth are complex, but the experience that other countries have had with public maintenance of drug-dependent persons, together with the artificially inflated prices that illegality imposes and the politically corrupting influence of the huge sums of money that are involved, all suggest that it is counterproductive to leave monopolistic control of production and distribution of now-illicit drugs in the hands of criminal entrepreneurs.

The fallacy of such action, or inaction, has driven many to contemplate appropriate terms for an armistice in the war on drugs. Specific details can be worked out later, but if we turn our attention to natural experiments as they occur in cross-cultural experience, the broad outlines of crucial first steps appear clear.

EUROPEAN EXPERIMENTS

One of the leading nations in the liberalization of drug laws is The Netherlands, in keeping with a governing principle of their public health system: Minimize harm. They still distinguish between "hard" and "soft" drugs and actively restrict traffic in "hard" drugs, but they recognize that those who need hard drugs should not be driven into the underworld in order to survive. Heroin and cocaine are available, at reasonable prices and with hygienic apparatuses, in government clinics. Although the sale of marijuana by unlicensed individuals is still illegal—to curb "pushers" who profit from engaging new users—anyone may buy it in the many coffeeshops that are designated outlets, which are marked by a discreet silhouette of a leaf displayed in a window. The Dutch system is not libertarian, as it is often mislabeled; half of those in prison are there on drug charges. Neither is the country encouraging a generation of drop-outs. The Netherlands has become a favorite hangout for expatriates from around the world, but, contrary to dire predictions, its drug policy, in combination with easy availability of treatment, has resulted in a reduction rather than an increase in the number of addicts. The Dutch also have much lower rates of incidence of overdose and of HIV seropositivity in comparison with the United States. . . .

On a smaller scale, a program in Liverpool continues to do much to normalize the lives of addicts by making drugs available at a clinic under safe conditions and with the encouragement of self-help group therapy and other treatments, which appear to be enjoying at least as much success as freestanding programs. In such a situation, addicts can hold regular jobs and take part in a wide range of community activities that would be closed to them in a context of prohibition. In a way, the Liverpool alternative is not markedly different from methadone maintenance that is offered at many places in the United States. No one doubts that methadone is addictive in the sense of creating a regular craving and psychological dependence; users suffer classic withdrawal syndrome if they are deprived of it too long. But it is a legally controlled drug, doled out regularly at clinics around the country and widely accepted as preferable to heroin, which remains prohibited. The dubious logic of this licit–illicit (or "soft"–"hard") drug distinction has been challenged by spokespersons for many minority groups who resent state-supported alternative addiction at a time when they are told that funds for treatment are not available even while facilities have long waiting lists of those who want to rehabilitate themselves.

LIBERALIZATION OF DRUG LAWS

Legalization of drugs need not be viewed as a single giant step in which all restrictions are abruptly removed, resulting in a chaotic free market. Again, the parallel with the repeal of national prohibition on alcohol is relevant. The federal government retained some oversight over production, quality control, and so forth, and levied a tax on both fermented beverages (wines, beers, ales, and related drinks) and distilled spirits (or "hard liquor"). A remarkable degree of discretion was given to the individual states, some of which further allowed for "local option" at a lower level. Even so, alcohol remains one of the most regulated products available, in terms of licensing, location, time, pricing, advertising, and other respects. Similar liberalization—with taxation and other regulation—could be tried for other drugs by various states.

In any such program, realistic education about alcohol and drugs and the outcomes of their use should be a cornerstone. The salutary experience of the Framingham, Massachusetts, heart-health study . . . and of a related study in Pawtucket, Rhode Island, demonstrates that public education can be immensely effective in promoting salubrious changes in behavior, despite the skepticism voiced by many in the drug field. The discrepancy probably results from a narrow interpretation of education, as if it were restricted to material taught in the classroom, often by individuals who are neither knowledgeable nor particularly interested in the subject. When serious efforts are made to educate an entire community, however, engaging grocery stores, scout groups, civil action organizations, churches, and other institutions as well as schools and the media, abundant knowledge can be effectively communicated in ways that affect attitudes and behavior, which in turn result in significant changes in the incidence and prevalence of various illnesses and other health problems.

EXPERIMENTS ARE NEEDED

The futility of the drug war in its present mode—both abroad and on the home front—suggests that it is time to call an armistice. Continuing legal prohibition as the major strategy for combating drugs is to attempt the impossible, by means that have already been discredited. Historical and cross-cultural evidence suggests that a wiser course would be to aim for a realistic accommodation, to permit but discourage risky misadventures by means that have already proven their effectiveness. This would not mean "surrender" to "the drug lords," nor would it usher in a period of reckless anarchy. Perhaps it would be less threatening to the narcomilitary complex if we were to speak in terms of "liberalization," rather than legalization, relegalization, or decriminalization. To allow people legal access to a substance does not mean that they need have unrestricted access to unlimited quantities. It might even be feasible for different jurisdictions to set up some natural experiments by adopting different specific regulations within a broad pattern of liberalization. In that way, we could soon expect at least quasiscientific evaluations of the outcomes, valuable information that could eventually serve as substantive data for making more confident choices among alternatives, in terms of public health and social welfare, as well as efficiency and efficacy. Instead of suffering a defeat, it could well be that such actions would, in the long run, signal a major victory for the people who are always the ones to suffer most in any kind of war.

PERIODICAL BIBLIOGRAPHY

The following articles have been selected to supplement the diverse views presented in this chapter. Addresses are provided for periodicals not indexed in the *Readers' Guide to Periodical Literature*, the *Alternative Press Index*, the *Social Sciences Index*, or the *Index to Legal Periodicals and Books*.

William J. Bennett	"We're Losing the Drug War," *World* & I, June 1995. Available from 3600 New York Ave. NE, Washington, DC 20002.
Eva Bertram and Kenneth Sharpe	"War Ends, Drugs Win," *Nation*, January 6, 1997.
William J. Chambliss	"Another Lost War: The Costs and Consequences of Drug Prohibition," *Social Justice*, Summer 1995.
Richard Cohen	"A Crusade That Spreads Corruption," *Washington Post*, March 10, 1996. Available from 1150 15th St. NW, Washington, DC 20071.
Craig Horowitz	"The No-Win War and Its Discontents," *New York*, February 5, 1996.
In These Times	"The Lost Cause," February 19, 1996.
Robert L. Maginnis	"How to Win the Drug War," *World* & I, December 1996.
Joseph McNamara	"The Drug War: Violent, Corrupt, and Unsuccessful," *Vital Speeches of the Day*, March 26, 1997.
National Review	"The War on Drugs Is Lost," special section, February 12, 1996.
George Soros	"Why the Drug War Cannot Be Won," *Washington Post National Weekly Edition*, February 10–16, 1997. Available from 1150 15th St. NW, Washington, DC 20071.
Jann S. Wenner and Ethan A. Nadelmann	"Clinton's War on Drugs: Cruel, Wrong, Unwinnable," *Rolling Stone*, April 17, 1997.
Gordon Witkin	"Why This Country Is Losing the Drug War," *U.S. News & World Report*, September 16, 1996.

WHICH CURRENT POLICIES ARE WORKING IN THE WAR ON DRUGS?

CHAPTER PREFACE

The war on drugs in the United States is being waged simultaneously on two main fronts: One prong attempts to interdict and disrupt the supply of drugs; the other aims to reduce the demand for drugs by users. Attacking the supply of drugs can involve such tactics as increased border patrol activity, harsher sentences for drug trafficking, and attempts to control the production of harmful drugs in foreign countries. Combating the demand for drugs includes such diverse approaches as tougher prosecution of illegal drug users and increased funding for drug education and treatment programs. A great deal of debate centers on whether supply-centered or demand-centered approaches are more effective at fighting drugs.

The usefulness of each of these approaches has come under attack in recent years; the drug education strategy is a case in point. The Drug Abuse Resistance Education (DARE) program is the most widely used school-based drug education program in the United States. In recent years, several studies have questioned the effectiveness of this program. Summing up one such study, James Bovard concludes that "DARE was found to deter drug, alcohol, or tobacco use in only a statistically insignificant three percent of program participants." Yet this program remains the cornerstone of the federal drug education strategy.

In a similar fashion, drug interdiction efforts have come under increased scrutiny in recent years, even as this strategy absorbs nearly 2 billion dollars annually in federal funds. The assumption behind interdiction is that the confiscation of illegal drugs will keep the price of drugs high, thus decreasing the number of those who can afford to use them. Critics of this policy, such as Kenneth E. Sharpe, contend that the price of drugs has been declining steadily in spite of increased funding for interdiction efforts. He argues that interdiction "never will succeed in limiting supply or raising prices enough to reduce use and abuse." Yet another point of view on this policy maintains that interdiction efforts are failing, but only because they are inadequately funded. Increased spending on interdiction, in this view, can produce the desired result of a reduction in drug use.

Each of these strategies in the war on drugs has its advocates and opponents, as the following chapter on current policies in the war on drugs will amply illustrate.

> "We must provide sufficient space in our prisons so that these repeat and violent criminals can be incapacitated for much longer sentences than are now being imposed."

INCARCERATION IS AN EFFECTIVE STRATEGY IN THE WAR ON DRUGS

Richard K. Willard

Many commentators argue that the strict arrest and sentencing policies of the war on drugs have crowded the nation's prisons with minor drug offenders. However, in the following viewpoint, Richard K. Willard, a lawyer and former assistant attorney general, contends that the vast majority of imprisoned drug offenders are incarcerated due to drug trafficking and violence, not casual use. He concludes that rather than reducing penalties for drug offenses, the nation should build more prisons and institute harsher sentences for drug crimes.

As you read, consider the following questions:

1. What is the flaw in the Justice Department study that calls 21 percent of prisoners "drug offenders," in Willard's view?
2. According to the author, how does the secrecy surrounding juvenile arrest and convictions skew the criminal justice statistics?
3. What percentage of prisoners in state prisons are first-time drug offenders, according to Willard?

From Richard K. Willard, "There Is No Alternative to Building More Prisons," *American Enterprise*, May/June 1995. Reprinted with permission of the *American Enterprise*, a Washington, D.C.–based magazine of politics, business, and culture.

M any violent criminals are turned loose today after serving amazingly lenient sentences. This has led to calls for building more prisons so that repeat violent offenders can be locked up for longer terms. Balancing this is a persistent question about whether our current prison capacity is being used properly. Some critics contend that our prisons contain substantial numbers of minor offenders, especially ones convicted of drug crimes, who can safely be released without endangering our communities. Before spending billions of dollars on new cells, they assert, we should make better use of existing space by reducing or eliminating sentences for these "non-threatening" felons.

Some of these critics cite a 1994 Justice Department study that indicated 21 percent of federal prisoners are "low-level drug offenders." The problems riddling this study start with its use of the euphemism "drug offender." In practice, virtually all of these federal prisoners were convicted of drug trafficking. These are not otherwise law-abiding citizens who happened to get nabbed for casual drug use. They are dealers.

VIOLENCE AND DRUGS

Drug dealing is a serious crime. Drug dealers destroy neighborhoods. They enmesh children in their illegal distribution networks, and peddle their poisons to all. Most drug dealers use violence as part of their trade. They often carry firearms, almost always illegally. A majority of all homicides today are drug-related.

Even if one believes that some drug dealers don't deserve prison terms, the Justice Department study seriously overstates the number of federal prisoners who could be considered non-threatening to their communities. Its list of "low-level offenders" includes many with prior records of serious criminal misconduct. The study's screening protocol was supposed to eliminate offenders with a history of violent crime, but further analysis showed that a significant percentage of persons charged with crimes of violence got through. Moreover, many of those with "non-violent" records had been charged with such serious felonies as burglary, a crime that certainly is a serious threat to community safety. In addition, 45 percent of the first-offender drug traffickers the study presents as candidates for release are non-U.S. citizens—and no consideration was given to whether these individuals might have prior criminal records abroad, and so not even be first offenders at all.

Another factor bedeviling the study's claim to have identified a large population of non-threatening prisoners is the fact that many records of juvenile arrests and convictions—even for the most serious violent crimes—are sealed or expunged and thus unavailable to researchers. Many a putative first offender actually has a lengthy record of prior criminal conduct as a juvenile. It is quite predictable that most of those convicts will commit violent and predatory crimes as soon as they are released.

A SMALL PROPORTION OF PRISONERS

A more fundamental problem with using this study to argue that our prisons contain significant numbers of harmless individuals is this: the Justice Department research covered only the federal prison system—which contains less than 7 percent of the country's total prison population. And, unlike their federal counterparts, only a small proportion of state prisoners are drug criminals. There are just 27,000 first-time drug offenders in state prisons today—less than 4 percent of the total state prison population.

MORE PRISONERS ARE NEEDED

The typical guy in prison has committed 15 serious crimes a year. Putting away 1,000 extra bad guys for a year reduces the expected number of murders by four, rapes by 53, assaults by 1,200, robberies by 1,100, burglaries by 2,600, auto thefts by 700, and other larcenies by 9,200.

The economics of putting people away are attractive. Incarceration costs around $33,000 a year, while estimates of the monetary and quality-of-life costs of crime—admittedly tougher to calculate—average around $60,000. We need more prisoners.

Daniel Seligman, Fortune, November 11, 1996.

It is thus hard to see how our states could free up much prison capacity by adopting more lenient sentencing policies for drug offenders. The vast proportion of first-time drug offenders already receive pretrial diversion, probation, or short sentences in local jails only. Among all drug offenders who go to state prison—including many repeat offenders—the median time actually served behind bars is only 12 months.

LONGER SENTENCES NEEDED

It is certainly true that we should optimize our use of limited and costly prison capacity. And it may be possible to release some small number of prisoners following drug treatment. In such cases, there should be frequent drug testing backed up by mandatory incarceration if drug use persists.

Reducing drug sentences, however, will not solve our shortage of prison capacity. In state and federal penitentiaries alike, most prisoners have long histories of antisocial criminal conduct. Huge numbers are chronic offenders. These are people who are unlikely to be rehabilitated, and releasing them will only increase victimization and crime losses across the larger society. We must provide sufficient space in our prisons so that these repeat and violent criminals can be incapacitated for much longer sentences than are now being imposed—not shorter ones.

> "[Federal antidrug laws] have functioned as a kind of giant vacuum cleaner hovering over the nation's inner cities, sucking young black men off the street and into prison."

INCARCERATION IS A COUNTERPRODUCTIVE AND RACIST STRATEGY

David T. Courtwright

In the following viewpoint, David T. Courtwright cites statistics showing that blacks are arrested and convicted for drug offenses at a dramatically higher rate than are whites. He contends that the policy of imprisoning large numbers of young black males, especially for minor drug offenses, is unjust, has failed to stem drug trafficking, and has devastated family life in black communities. Courtwright is professor of history and health sciences at the University of North Florida and the author of *Violent Land: Single Men and Social Disorder from the Frontier to the Inner City.*

As you read, consider the following questions:

1. According to Courtwright, why does the rate of illegitimate births rise when marriageable women greatly outnumber marriageable men?
2. Why, according to the author, do police claim it is more convenient to arrest black drug offenders than white offenders?
3. What is one of the drug policy reforms endorsed by the author?

Reprinted, with permission, from David T. Courtwright, "The Drug War's Hidden Toll," *Issues in Science and Technology*, Winter 1996–97, pp. 71–77. Copyright 1997 by the University of Texas at Dallas, Richardson, Texas.

The root cause of crime, or at any rate violent crime, is the failure of families to shape and restrain the behavior of young men, who are responsible for much more than their share of murders, robberies, and other serious offenses. Yet not all young men are criminally inclined. Those who are raised in intact families and who then marry and become parents themselves, thereby acquiring a familial stake and the responsibilities that go with it, do not require expensive legal deterrence (or medical treatment) as often as those who do not. Societies that attempt to control behavior by relying on police and prisons rather than families have more crime and heavier taxes, plus ever larger outlays for private security. The great fiscal virtue of attentive parenting and matrimonial stability is that they are by far the cheapest way to maintain social order.

Heavy reliance on the criminal justice system can also reach the point where it undermines family life. Imprisoning a large number of men distorts the marriage market and thereby increases the likelihood of illegitimacy and discourages the formation of families. This is especially true for groups that have low gender ratios, the most important group being blacks in inner cities. Criminal justice reform—in particular, reform of drug laws and drug enforcement tactics—can help to restore balance to the black marriage market. Making the number of marriageable black men and women more nearly equal is a necessary, though not a sufficient, condition for a long-term reduction in the high levels of criminal violence and social disorder that plague U.S. inner cities. . . .

MASS INCARCERATION AND ITS COSTS

But marriage and family formation are not simply a function of the raw gender ratio. To be eligible for marriage, a young man has to be in circulation, not locked away somewhere. Yet by 1995, one of every three black American men in their twenties, the prime age for marriage, was in prison, on probation, or on parole. By comparison, only about one black woman in 20 was in similar straits.

Let's look more closely at the numbers. On any given day in 1994, more than 787,000 black men in their twenties were under some form of criminal justice control. Of these, 306,000 were behind bars; 351,000 on probation; and 130,000 on parole. An unknown but not inconsiderable number were hiding from arrest warrants. The cost to taxpayers for the criminal justice control of these black men is more than $6 billion per year. Of course, those among them who are behind bars are not committing street crimes. . . . Indeed, some observers think that the mass incarceration of young black men is what is behind the decline in violent crime rates in the past five years. Other theorists have stressed the progressive aging of the baby boomers; a temporary (and soon-to-be-reversed) decline in the relative number of teenagers; a healthier economy; the stabilization of urban drug markets; more aggressive police tactics; the proliferation of trauma centers (which, by saving more gunshot victims, lowers the homicide rate); and the notion that the number of violent crimes has, in some neighborhoods, fallen below an epidemic "tipping point." None of these theories is exclusive of the others.

RACE AND THE WAR ON DRUGS

The "war on drugs" launched in the mid-1980s was a pivotal event in the history of African-American imprisonment in the United States. Amid much media fanfare, President Reagan launched the war on drugs by saying, "The American people want their government to get tough and go on the offensive." He promised that police would attack the drug problem "with more ferocity than ever before." What he did not say was that *police enforcement of new drug laws would focus almost exclusively on low-level dealers in minority neighborhoods.* Police found more drugs in minority communities because that is where they looked for them. Had they pointed the drug war at college campuses, it is likely that our jails would now be filled overwhelmingly with university students.

African-American arrest rates for drugs during the height of the "drug war" in 1989 were five times higher than arrest rates for whites *even though whites and African-Americans were using drugs at the same rate.* African-Americans make up 12 percent of the U.S. population and constitute 13 percent of all monthly drug users, but represent 35 percent of those arrested for drug possession, 55 percent of those convicted of drug possession, and 74 percent of those sentenced to prison for drug possession. While the rhetoric of the drug war may have peaked, the particular "practice" of the drug war still is being carried out with considerable vigor.

Steven R. Donziger, *The Real War on Crime.* New York: HarperPerennial, 1996.

Yet even if mass incarceration turns out to be causally related to the recent decline in violent crime rates, we need to consider its long-term social costs. The doubling of the inmate population since 1985 has diverted dollars from education, particularly state-supported higher education. Inflation-adjusted funding per credit hour has eroded as penal outlays have increased, thereby diminishing young people's future employment (and hence marital) prospects.

Children whose parents are in jail have suffered. More than 60 percent of male inmates have children, legitimate or otherwise, and most of those children are under 18. The absence of their fathers and whatever financial and emotional support they might have provided does not improve their life prospects. Neither do their parents' criminal records. Marc Mauer and Tracy Huling of The Sentencing Project in Washington, D.C., who assembled the black prison numbers, have argued that young men who have done time are at an economic and marital disadvantage when released. In a sense, they take their bars with them. A prior criminal record reduces their chance of finding gainful employment, making them less attractive as marriage partners and less able to provide for their children.

Fewer Marriageable Men

The most subtle effect of the prison boom, however, has been the unintended lowering of the ratio of marriageable men to women, particularly, as we have seen, in the black community, where young men are less numerous to begin with. The smaller the ratio, the greater men's sexual bargaining power and hence the likelihood of illegitimacy and single-parent families, which are the root causes of violence and disorder in the inner city. The solution makes the problem circular.

This doesn't mean that we should tear down the prisons, but it does mean that we should think carefully about how and why these resources are used. The drug war, the single most important reason for the increasing rate of imprisonment among young black men, is the obvious place to begin.

The Drug War's Toll

First, there is the problem of racial bias in drug arrests, prosecutions, and sentencing. In 1992, blacks made up about 12 percent of the U.S. population and, according to the National Household Survey on Drug Abuse, about 13 percent of those who reported using any illicit drug on a monthly basis. Yet more than a third of all drug possession arrests, more than half of all possession convictions, and three-quarters of state prison sentences for possession involved blacks.

In Georgia, where the organization Human Rights Watch has made a detailed study, more whites than blacks were arrested for drug offenses before the drug war began in the mid-1980s. By the end of the decade, blacks were arrested for drug offenses more than twice as often as whites, even though blacks made up less than a third of the population. From 1990 through 1995, the black drug arrest rate per 100,000 was more than five times that of whites.

For sale or possession of marijuana, blacks were arrested at roughly twice the rate of white Georgians. For cocaine possession, blacks were arrested at a rate 16 times that of whites; for cocaine sale, 21 times. Marijuana and cocaine use and sale were more widespread in the black community, but the arrest rates were well beyond anything suggested by national prevalence data. Between 1991 and 1994, blacks made up from 14 to 18 percent of marijuana users and 18 to 38 percent of cocaine users, according to statistics that Human Rights Watch derived from the National Household Survey on Drug Abuse.

A MATTER OF CONVENIENCE

The arrest-rate disparity was partly a matter of convenience. Black users and dealers, who often sell outdoors and to strangers, were more visible and easier to arrest in street sweeps. "When you want to catch fish," explained one Georgia official, requesting anonymity, "you go where the fishing is easiest." The pond, however, is so well stocked that the fishing has little effect: Lower-level black cocaine dealers are easily and quickly replaced. Indeed, they have been known to "drop a dime" on their rivals simply to eliminate competition and expand their own turf.

Though wholesale black arrests for cocaine dealing have not stopped street trafficking, they most assuredly have had an impact on the black male inmate population, beginning with the local lockup. A study of 150,000 criminal cases in Connecticut found that bail for black and Hispanic men averaged twice that of whites for the same offense. Those who could not afford the higher rates stayed in jail. Nor did their chances improve in the pretrial phase. A California study of 700,000 cases found that blacks and Hispanics were less likely than whites to have their charges dropped or cases dismissed, to plead out cheaply, or otherwise benefit from prosecutorial or judicial discretion.

A POLICY FIASCO

But the most conspicuous (and correctable) problem is that federal and many state laws make even small-time drug dealing a big-time offense carrying a stiff sentence. This is especially true of crack, the drug war's bête noir. In 1986, Congress enacted a sentencing provision that required only 1/100 of the amount of crack cocaine to trigger the same penalty as powder cocaine. Deal 500 grams of powder cocaine, get five years; deal five grams of crack, ditto. The result was that, by 1993, federal prison sentences for blacks averaged 41 percent longer than those of whites, with the crack/powder distinction being the major reason for the difference. Pharmacologically absurd and racially unjust on the face of it, the 100-to-1 ratio has been a policy fiasco of the first magnitude, compounded by Congress's politically motivated refusal to heed the U.S. Sentencing Commission's advice to drop it.

This criticism should not be confused with a call for legalization. The original point of the drug war, which began in 1986, was to mount a high-visibility campaign, orchestrated by the White House, to restrict and stigmatize drug use through increased education, prevention, treatment, and enforcement efforts. This was a reasonable goal and met with some success, notably among young people and adults who use drugs only occasionally. In the 1990s, the drug war's leadership and moral purpose have disappeared, and education, prevention, and treatment dollars are harder to come by. That has left as the drug war's principal enduring legacy the harshest penal aspects of the 1986 and 1988 federal antidrug laws. Intentionally or not, these laws and their state equivalents have functioned as a kind of giant vacuum cleaner hovering over the nation's inner cities, sucking young black men off the street and into prison. More rational, flexible, and fiscally prudent state and federal sentencing policies within the context of a balanced drug war—the prescription of a majority of the nation's police chiefs—would help to redress the scarcity of marriageable black men and other long-term problems associated with mass incarceration. . . .

CRIMINAL JUSTICE REFORMS NEEDED

Sending fewer black men to prison is not going to solve the problem by itself. Black families are in trouble for many reasons, among them labor-market changes, a legacy of welfare dependency, racial and class segregation, and the inversion of traditional values, both within the street culture of the ghetto and the larger, eroticized, commercial culture of the mass media. It isn't enough to keep young men eligible for marriage by keeping them out of jail. They also need jobs and the will to keep at those jobs and to base family life on them.

Yet there is good statistical evidence that the low ratio of marriageable black males to females, exacerbated by the drug war and the sentencing revolution of the 1980s and 1990s, has encouraged illegitimacy and family disruption. Robert Sampson, who analyzed census data from 171 cities, found that "the strongest predictor by far" of black family disruption was the gender ratio, followed by black male employment. Family disruption, Sampson hypothesized, gives rise to violence, which reduces the effective gender ratio directly (census takers don't count dead men) and indirectly through imprisonment, which simultaneously hurts male job prospects.

The crime and violence stemming from family disruption have not only landed more young black men in prison or the morgue, they have landed more law-and-order politicians in office—another and by no means the least way in which the problem has become circular. Since 1980, if not before, the electoral dividends of appearing tough on crime have been more appealing to U.S. politicians than the long-term social dividends of flexible and reasonable criminal sanctions. Getting rid of the 100-to-1 ratio; revising sentencing guidelines to permit greater judicial discretion, including referral of more drug users into treatment; eliminating mandatory minimum sentences for lower-level trafficking offenses—these and other reforms will require real political courage. This is especially so because criminal justice reform is no panacea. It is best understood as a necessary though not sufficient condition for the long-term diminishment of violence and disorder in the inner cities, America's new violent frontiers.

| "Expanding treatment would be a constructive step toward easing this nation's drug problem."

DRUG ABUSE TREATMENT PROGRAMS ARE EFFECTIVE

Jonathan P. Caulkins

In the following viewpoint, Jonathan P. Caulkins contends that, even though drug treatment programs achieve low rates of complete abstinence, they are still the most cost-effective way to reduce drug consumption. The law enforcement approach, including interdiction and incarceration, must spend far more money to achieve similar rates of reduced consumption, according to Caulkins. Drug treatment programs do not have to be perfect, in the author's view, in order to provide valuable benefits to society. Caulkins is codirector of the RAND Drug Policy Research Center and a professor at Carnegie-Mellon University.

As you read, consider the following questions:

1. What is the "during treatment" effect that Caulkins thinks is often ignored?
2. What does the author mean when he calls drug treatment an "investment in human capital"?
3. How does treatment for drug users help the noncriminals around that user, according to Caulkins?

The story Thomas tells is poignant: "I was a full-blown addict by 1987 and started to get into trouble with my family. I kept spending all our money on my drugs. By 1989 I had depleted all of our funds and started to sell my material possessions. I had also started stealing to support my habit. . . . I was sent to a drug and alcohol treatment program almost two years ago. It has saved my life."

Mary cannot tell her own story. She came from an alcoholic family, began using illicit drugs at age 11, was smoking crack by 15 and first injected heroin at age 17. Mary entered and completed a residential treatment program but still continued to abuse drugs and commit crime. She was imprisoned at 20 and died of an overdose a day after she was released.

Do drug-treatment programs work? As these vignettes from recent reports on treatment efficacy show, a fair answer is "sometimes." A wiser answer is, "It depends on how you define 'works.'"

Treatment is not a magic bullet that prevents every client from ever relapsing to drug use; indeed, the majority of users do relapse. But treatment works very well in other senses of the word, including some that are highly relevant to the current debate about treatment funding.

Consider a recent study conducted by Peter Rydell and Susan Everingham of RAND's Drug Policy Research Center. The researchers assumed that each time 100 heavy cocaine users enter a treatment program, only 13 percent of them reduce their use in the long run because of that episode of treatment. For 87 percent of the users, treatment was either not needed or brought, at most, temporary benefits.

COST-EFFECTIVE RESULTS

Nevertheless, the study found treating heavy cocaine users to be a very cost-effective way to reduce consumption—seven times more cost-effective than the best enforcement program directed at controlling the supply of cocaine. Let's say the goal is to reduce U.S. cocaine consumption by 1 percent on average during the next 15 years. That could be accomplished by upgrading efforts to control cocaine production in South America—at an estimated additional cost of almost $800 million per year. Or that same reduction could be achieved by spending more on interdicting cocaine at the border—$350 million more per year; or by spending more to arrest, convict and incarcerate drug sellers within the United States—costing an additional $250 million per year. Or, the United States could spend just $34 million per year more to expand treatment for heavy users.

In other words, while expanding any of these programs would reduce cocaine use, expanding treatment is a far cheaper way to accomplish the reduction.

The RAND study found that treatment was absolutely, as well as relatively, cost-effective in the following sense. Spending money on treatment reduces cocaine use. Reducing cocaine use reduces drug-related societal costs. For example, drug addicts who steal to support their habits commit fewer crimes while in treatment, and they are less likely to report to hospital emergency rooms with drug-related complications. Updating health economist Dorothy Rice's 1990 estimates of the costs drugs impose on American society, the RAND study estimated that every dollar spent treating heavy cocaine users averts more than $7 in measurable social costs (criminal justice budgets, lost worker productivity, health care expenditures, etc.), as well as an immeasurable amount of pain and suffering.

Cheaper than Enforcement

The RAND study's conclusion that only 13 percent of people entering a treatment program reduce their drug use in the long run because of that episode of treatment is a conservative estimate, but it turns out that treatment still would be more cost-effective than the supply-control programs, even if the long-term effect were assumed to be zero. Just the short-run reduction in consumption while a client is actually in treatment makes treatment cheaper than enforcement.

Evaluations of treatment regularly ignore the during-treatment effect and focus entirely on how many clients remain abstinent thereafter. This is ironic, because the opposite approach is common in criminal-justice studies which often assume that there is no rehabilitation and that the only positive benefit is incarceration while the person is in the system.

Even if treatment and the supply-control programs were equally cost-effective in terms of ability to reduce cocaine consumption per dollar of government spending, there are other reasons to increase our emphasis on the former.

Treatment Reduces Demand

First, treatment is better at slowing the cash flow into drug markets and, hence, reducing associated crime and violence. Many of the dollars spent on cocaine are the proceeds of property crime and become black-market revenues that drug dealers fight over—with dire consequences for them and for innocent bystanders. Since treatment reduces demand—which generally depresses prices—it reduces drug spending by an even greater amount than it reduces consumption. In contrast, most supply-side interventions raise the cost of supplying drugs, driving up prices. So when enforcement suppresses consumption, drug spending, with its associated property and violent crime, does not fall as fast. If the demand for drugs is what economists call "relatively inelastic," then increasing enforcement actually can increase the dollar value of the drug market.

REFERRALS TO TREATMENT REDUCE ABUSE

Criminal justice referral to treatment relieves courts and prisons of overcrowding and reduces the high cost of continued incarceration, while providing an added degree of supervision beyond what probation or parole offices may be able to afford. When successful, treatment further reduces the criminal justice costs by breaking the pattern of recidivism that brings typical substance abusers back into the criminal justice system again and again. Research on criminal-justice involved populations suggests that substance abuse treatment can be effective in reducing substance abuse and criminal activity while the client is in treatment and for some time thereafter.

Sharron Kelley, "Effectiveness of Drug Treatment as an Alternative to Jail" (memorandum posted on World Wide Web), October 24, 1995.

Second, interactions between the markets for different drugs can undermine the effectiveness of enforcement. Successfully treating someone whose primary addiction is to cocaine may lead that person to consume less of other drugs as well. In contrast, when arresting cocaine suppliers drives up cocaine prices, the resulting reduction in cocaine use comes about, in part, because users shift from cocaine to other drugs such as amphetamines or heroin.

Third, treatment brings other social benefits, whereas drug enforcement brings other social costs. Many treatment programs not only reduce drug use, but also teach life skills such as financial management and parenting, offer job training and career counseling, help clients obtain a GED, provide family counseling and so on. In short, treatment is an investment in human capital. In contrast, a felony record for narcotics violations can make an already marginalized individual essentially unemployable.

Treatment is not only smart, it's also necessary. The RAND study projected what would happen to cocaine consumption during the next 15 years if current policies are continued. Assuming we can keep initiation into cocaine use low, the number of users will fall. But the reduction will come primarily among light, not compulsive, users. Unless something is done to address the more than 2 million current heavy users, the quantity of cocaine sold and consumed will decline much more slowly than will the number of users.

Despite this evidence, treatment remains unpopular, receiving only about $2.6 billion of the $13.2 billion the federal government spent on drug control in 1995, and a much smaller fraction of the larger amount spent at the state and local level. Some of the resistance comes from people who do not realize that a highly imperfect program—even one with a 13 percent success rate—can be a prudent investment and sound policy. Some of the resistance is familiar local politics; few people want a treatment facility in their neighborhood.

RELUCTANCE TO HELP CRIMINALS

The more fundamental problem, though, seems to be a reluctance to use tax dollars to help criminals. Such reluctance is not unreasonable when budget cuts threaten good programs in which the direct beneficiaries are upstanding citizens. Still, treatment also helps noncriminals. When heavy users reduce or stop using drugs they become better parents, they are more likely to be employed, they reduce or stop victimizing others to raise money for drugs and they stop supporting a violent black market. It would be tragic if moral outrage against helping drug users were to prevent the government from protecting law-abiding citizens from crime and violence. Nonusers do not have to be saints or altruists to support treatment—just frugal taxpayers who are worried about crime.

None of this should, in any way, be construed as saying that enforcement is not needed. Far from it. Indeed, drug treatment derives some of its effectiveness from the threat of tough enforcement. Efforts to reduce or control the supply of drugs make them expensive, more difficult to find and risky to buy or possess. These penalties give users an incentive to seek treatment. Enforcement also can complement treatment more directly. Drug courts give arrested users the option of entering treatment; those who opt for treatment are monitored through drug testing, and failed tests lead to incarceration.

EASING THE DRUG PROBLEM

It also must be noted that expanding treatment, although wise, is not a complete answer. The RAND study predicts that even if every heavy cocaine user were offered treatment once each year, even after 15 years consumption would only be cut in half. Hence, in addition to expanding treatment, we need to look for ways to quickly reduce those forms of drug use that have the worst consequences for society in general and for the users themselves.

Nevertheless, treatment works—not perfectly, but well enough. For every Thomas there may be a Mary, or two, or seven. But solid research shows there are enough people like Thomas that expanding treatment would be a constructive step toward easing this nation's drug problem.

"We do not know that drug abuse treatment is effective."

DRUG ABUSE TREATMENT HAS NOT BEEN PROVEN EFFECTIVE

Robert Apsler

In recent years, government funding for drug abuse treatment has increased, and many critics of the war on drugs think it should be increased even further. In the following viewpoint, Robert Apsler, an assistant professor of psychology in the Department of Psychiatry at Harvard Medical School, challenges this emerging consensus, contending that there is no solid evidence that drug abuse treatment is effective. Apsler suggests that spending vast sums of money on programs that have not been proven useful may be premature. Although he concedes that some programs appear effective for drug abusers who sincerely want treatment, Apsler contends that a very small fraction of drug abusers fit this description.

As you read, consider the following questions:

1. What are the two competing definitions of "effective" drug abuse treatment, according to the author?
2. According to Apsler, what percentage of those suffering from alcoholism or alcohol problems are able to recover on their own?
3. What usually happens, in Apsler's view, when drug abusers enter drug abuse treatment against their wishes?

From Robert Apsler, "Is Drug Abuse Treatment Effective?" *American Enterprise*, March/April 1994. Reprinted with permission of the *American Enterprise*, a Washington, D.C.–based magazine of politics, business, and culture.

In early February 1994, the Clinton administration spelled out its national antidrug strategy. Much of the debate over [this] program will turn on how much federal support should be made available for treating drug addicts. The administration plans to spend $355 million in new grants for the states to use to treat hardcore drug users, while cutting funds for interdiction. Many years of massive federal investment in interdiction—including involvement of the U.S. military—have failed to reduce the availability of low-cost street drugs. And the policy momentum is now toward shifting federal funds from supply reduction to demand reduction, a move that would benefit treatment and prevention programs. Also, news stories about the administration's deliberations often report on drug treatment programs with long waits for new admissions. What is implied if not stated is that the size of the country's drug abusing population, estimated by the Institute of Medicine to be 5.5 million people, would be significantly reduced if more money were spent for drug abuse treatment.

But missing from the news stories and analyses of proposed antidrug strategies is any frank discussion of the underlying assumption that drug abuse treatment is effective. This assumption is based largely on reports from clinicians and recovered drug addicts. It is encouraged by a growing drug treatment industry and accepted by a public that wishes for a solution to the drug problem. The premise may be accurate, but it is not yet supported by hard evidence. We do not know that drug abuse treatment is effective. Clinicians' reports in other areas have not always been reliable. For example, many medical procedures developed through clinical experience alone have been abandoned when researchers showed, through carefully controlled comparisons, that placebos or other alternatives matched their effectiveness.

With a few exceptions, drug abuse treatment has not been subjected to rigorous tests for effectiveness. Good research doesn't exist for a number of reasons. Researchers are hampered by fundamental conceptual issues. Even defining basic ideas is difficult. There are significant practical obstacles that make conducting research difficult as well, and little federal support for drug treatment research has been available for over a decade. . . .

WHAT IS "EFFECTIVE" TREATMENT?

There [is no] agreed-upon definition of what constitutes *effective* drug abuse treatment. Definitions clash in two important ways. First, strongly held views divide the treatment community on whether abstinence from illicit drug use is necessary. One position holds that successful treatment is synonymous with total abstinence from illicit drugs. The other position holds that treatment is successful if it ends clients' *dependence* on drugs. Continued, moderate drug use is accepted for those clients able to gain control over their drug use and prevent it from interfering with their daily functioning.

Definitions of effectiveness also differ in the number of behaviors they measure. The most common view of effectiveness judges treatment by its ability to reduce the two behaviors most responsible for society's strong reaction against drug abuse: illicit drug use and criminal activity. Others argue that a broader definition of effectiveness is necessary to describe treatment accurately. Advocates of the broader definition believe that treatment should not be considered effective if it can only demonstrate reductions in drug use and illegal activity, since these changes are likely to dissipate rapidly unless clients undergo additional changes. Returning clients who have completed treatment to their previous drug using environment, it is argued, subjects them to the same social and economic forces that contributed to their drug use. According to this view, sustained changes occur only when clients are willing and able to survive and prosper in new environments. To do so, clients must first develop the necessary employment, social and other skills. Broad definitions of effectiveness usually include: (1) drug abuse, (2) illegal activities, (3) employment, (4) length of stay in treatment, (5) social functioning, (6) intrapersonal functioning, and (7) physical health and longevity.

MOTIVATION FOR TREATMENT

Without having resolved even basic definitions about drug abuse treatment, the administration is nevertheless proceeding on the assumption that more money for treatment will mean more help. Doing so ignores the fact that we don't know very much in this area and also ignores the little we do know. We don't know much about client differences, for instance. But we do know that a drug addict's motivation for seeking treatment is crucial. Most clinicians believe that successful treatment is impossible if a client does not want help. Addicts must admit the existence of a serious problem and sincerely want to do something about it. Only then will they accept the assistance of clinicians. However, most experts in the drug abuse field reluctantly acknowledge that almost no drug abusers actually *want* treatment. The news reports implying that thousands of needy addicts would enter treatment and soon be on their way to recovery if the country were willing to spend more money and increase the number of drug programs are inaccurate. While waiting lists exist for some programs, others have trouble attracting addicts.

TREATMENT IS A WASTE OF TIME

Drug czar [Barry McCaffrey] supplies no response to the criticism that treatment has proved a waste of time during the last two decades. A recent Rand Corp. study found that 87 percent of cocaine addicts who participate in treatment programs relapse and continue as heavy users. Recidivism rates also are high for heroin addicts. Why is the United States spending so much money on treatment that doesn't work? Is it because treatment advocates are efficient lobbyists, or is it the inevitable by-product of an administration that has a sixties-era mind-set that favors decriminalization?

Jamie Dettmer, *Insight*, March 31, 1997.

Furthermore, most drug abusers enter treatment when faced with a crisis, such as threats by a judge, employer, or spouse, or a combination of the three. As a result, the drug abuser's objective may be limited to overcoming the current problem. When the crisis has abated, patients often admit they do not intend all drug use to stop. A national survey of admissions to public drug programs from 1979 to 1981 found that pressure from the criminal justice system was the strongest motivation for seeking treatment. Thus, the existence of long waiting lists may tell us more about judges' efforts to find alternatives to incarceration in overcrowded jails than about the actual intentions of drug abusers or the effectiveness of treatment programs. . . .

RESEARCH DESIGN PROBLEMS

Questions about drug treatment effectiveness must be answered the same way as similar questions about treatments for the common cold, AIDS, or other ailments, that is, by obtaining evidence that compares the outcomes of treated and untreated individuals. While this may seem obvious, most drug treatment research has neither compared the necessary groups of drug users nor employed the types of research designs capable of producing strong conclusions. In addition, serious measurement and attrition problems weaken the conclusions of most studies of drug treatment effectiveness.

Comparisons between drug users who receive treatment and

others who do not are almost nonexistent. Researchers study only treated drug users. Yet the observed behavior of drug users who do not enter drug programs reinforces the need for researchers to include untreated addicts in their studies. We have known for years, for instance, that some drug abusers, including heroin addicts, end drug use largely on their own. Researchers have also observed large reductions in drug use among drug abusers waiting for, but not yet receiving, treatment for cocaine abuse.

The phenomenon of people ending their use of highly addictive *legal* substances on their own is well documented. For example, there is mounting evidence that smokers quit on their own at about the same rate as those attending smoking treatment programs. Estimates of remission from alcoholism and alcohol problems without formal treatment range from 45 to 70 percent. No comparable estimate is available for the number of drug users who quit on their own. Until we know the recovery rates for untreated drug abusers, it is impossible to claim that treatment is more effective than the absence of treatment.

Furthermore, the research designs and methods employed in most drug treatment research are so seriously flawed that the results can be considered no more than suggestive. Many investigations study a single group of treated clients and attempt to draw conclusions without a comparison group. Other investigations compare different groups of clients receiving different treatments. In nearly all such cases, the types of clients differ from group to group. Consequently, it is impossible to distinguish between effects caused by treatment differences and effects caused by client differences.

MEASURING THE OUTCOMES OF TREATMENT

One major need in drug treatment research is for an objective, reliable, and inexpensive method for measuring treatment outcomes. Presently most treatment researchers rely entirely on clients' own reports of past and current behavior. Much of the behavior that clients are asked about is illegal, occurred while they were intoxicated, and may have taken place months, and even years, earlier. As one would expect, clients underreport their drug use and other illegal activities. Yet the drug treatment field continues to rely heavily on these dubious reports because there are no suitable alternatives. Chemical tests, such as urine and hair testing, are important adjuncts for validating clients' reports. But at best these tests confirm use or abstinence; they do not indicate anything about quantity or intervals of use. So they are crude measures that cannot easily track patterns of drug use over long periods after a client leaves a treatment program.

Many treatment studies measure clients at the beginning and end of treatment because it is so difficult and expensive to keep track of them after they have completed a program. Some studies do attempt to assess the impact of treatment six months, a year, or even longer after completion. But investigators can seldom locate more than 70 percent of clients, if that. Clients who cannot be contacted are often deceased, in prison, unemployed, and/or homeless. Leaving them out of the studies may skew the findings, making the conclusions appear more positive than is warranted. . . .

Further Studies Needed

Drug abuse treatment features prominently in discussions of how the Clinton administration should respond to the country's concern about drug abuse. Yet little hard evidence documents the effectiveness of treatment. . . .

The absence of convincing evidence about the effectiveness of drug abuse treatment results from the lack of rigorous evaluations. Only a handful of randomized clinical trials have been conducted as of April 1994. More need to be done, and valid and comprehensive measures of treatment effectiveness need to be employed in these studies in order to end the reliance of treatment researchers on clients' self-reports of sensitive behaviors. Treatment research also needs more post-treatment follow-ups to show that treatment effects persist once clients leave their programs.

Finally, researchers must learn what happens to untreated drug abusers. Past and current research focuses almost exclusively on drug abusers who enter treatment. This research does not make comparisons between treated and untreated drug abusers and cannot answer the most fundamental question of all: is treatment more cost-effective than no treatment?

"[Interdiction] works . . . for the simple reason that it raises the cost to smugglers, increasing the cost of the illegal narcotics."

INTERDICTION OF THE DRUG SUPPLY REDUCES DRUG USE

Pamela Falk

Pamela Falk argues in the following viewpoint that the recent shift of resources from drug interdiction to drug abuse treatment has led to a major increase in drug trafficking. According to Falk, the flow of drugs into the United States can be seriously disrupted by a renewed emphasis on interdiction, especially at the nation's border with Mexico. Falk contends that a serious effort at interdiction will result in a reduction in drug use in the United States. Falk, a former staff director of the House Subcommittee on Western Hemisphere Affairs, is a professor at City University of New York School of Law.

As you read, consider the following questions:

1. According to Falk, what percentages of heroin and cocaine now enter the United States across the Mexican border?
2. What evidence does Falk provide to show that the United States and Mexico are losing the war on drugs?
3. What firearms policy concerning U.S. narcotics agents should be adopted, according to the author?

Reprinted from Pamela Falk, "Drugs Across the Border: A War We're Losing," *Washington Post*, September 29, 1997, by permission of the author.

The White House interim report on Mexico's efforts to fight drug trafficking characterized them as moderately successful. While the report properly cites cooperation and laws to monitor money laundering, it concedes that Mexican law enforcement has been penetrated by the cartels it seeks to destroy.

By underscoring the deployment of high-technology screening systems on the border and applauding Mexico's investigation of corrupt law enforcement and military officials, the administration and its Office of National Drug Control Policy have in fact reversed course: They have adopted an emphasis on the supply side of the drug war.

A SHIFT IN POLICY

The lesson of Clinton's first-term drug policy should by now be clear: Shifting resources away from seizures, as the president did back in 1993, caused Mexico to become the gateway for illegal drugs into the United States. Now a long-awaited shift has taken place, and the administration is, at least in its report to Congress, emphasizing a policy of interdiction: halting and seizing illegal drugs at the border. This works, if done as part of a serious comprehensive plan, for the simple reason that it raises the cost to smugglers, increasing the cost of the illegal narcotics. Consumption, as a direct result, decreases.

Studies exist on both sides of the divide over drug policy. A Rand report provided the basis for the administration's past shifting of significant resources from interdiction to treatment (or the demand side), even though a Defense Department report showed that interdiction worked to reduce drug use. But the evidence is overwhelming that the years 1994–1997 have seen a crisis-level increase in drug trafficking, with 70 percent of the cocaine and 30 percent of the heroin now entering the United States from Mexico.

Nevertheless the administration has chosen to certify Mexico as cooperating in the drug trafficking war. Despite evidence to the contrary, the White House decided to give Mexico the all-clear on certification not because it had improved its methods but because it was in the U.S. national interest to do so. Bilateral relations are not just about drugs and crime and they are not just about Washington and the Mexican government.

LOSING THE WAR

In fact, the United States and Mexico are losing the drug war. Over the summer of 1997, a wave of drug-related assassinations occurred, and the showcase for Mexico's drug control efforts,

Ciudad Juarez and the state of Chihuahua—in which the war on drugs was totally taken over from the police by the army—is now overrun with both drugs and homicides. Four Mexican drug rings smuggle between $10 billion and $30 billion worth of narcotics annually.

SUCCESSFUL INTERDICTION OF DRUG FLIGHTS

U.S. Customs have never claimed to have stopped 100 percent of the drug smuggling by air and doesn't believe that goal is achievable. Our goal from the outset has been to make such activity too risky for all but the most foolhardy smuggler. The effort has paid off, as Customs and its allies have reduced air intrusions into the United States by 75 percent to 80 percent of that experienced during the 1970s and 1980s.

Joseph W. Maxwell, *San Diego Union-Tribune*, October 12, 1997.

What can the United States do, without engendering animosity on the part of Mexico, to play a less passive role in a drug problem that is devastating that country? With the White House drug office up for evaluation for funding and some of the congressional critics somewhat assuaged by the focus on enforcement—particularly Sens. Paul Coverdell (R-Ga.) and Dianne Feinstein (D-Calif.)—the time is right to take the following approach:

• Interdiction of the flow of narcotics over both land and sea borders, an effort that should include cooperation by Mexico with U.S. counter-narcotics law enforcement. U.S. agents should be granted explicit permission by Mexico to carry sidearms on the Mexican side of the border. The "wink and nod" approach that many White House and law enforcement officials point to—that is, that many agents carry sidearms but official talk of it is unacceptable—is outdated. The approval should be formalized.

• Compliance by Mexico with long-standing extradition requests, most notably of traffickers, both Mexican nationals and American, who have been indicted in U.S. courts. This is something the president failed to secure during his trip to Mexico in May 1997.

MORE DIRECT INVOLVEMENT

• Creation of a more active and direct U.S. role in the Mexican money laundering investigations. The recent Mexican request to freeze a Citibank New York account that may hold Juarez cartel money is the first in a series of investigations that should be stepped up with U.S. help.

• Joint investigation and prosecution of the major drug cartels in Mexico. Congress has called for the development and strengthening of permanent working relationships between U.S. and Mexican law enforcement agencies. This is important, as is U.S. help in developing adequate screening processes to assess law enforcement officials on both sides of the border.

• Concentration of intelligence efforts that have ignored or missed vital information on corrupt antidrug enforcement officials. Repeated interagency fighting between the Justice Department and the FBI—with a bloated budget of $16 billion—has hampered efforts to clamp down in interdiction and extradition efforts. The White House office has failed to reduce the internecine battles that impede successful counter-narcotics moves.

The administration theme that drugs are a common enemy is a good one. Mexican citizens want to live drug-free, as do Americans. The answer lies, however, in getting rid of land mines, not tiptoeing through them.

"There is no evidence that increased drug interdiction has a meaningful effect on the price or even the overall availability of drugs."

INTERDICTION OF THE DRUG SUPPLY IS FUTILE

Kenneth E. Sharpe

In the following viewpoint, written just before the 1996 presidential election, Kenneth E. Sharpe argues that the virtues of the drug interdiction strategy are much exaggerated by political candidates and other proponents. Sharpe points out that the interdiction strategy has failed to achieve any of its goals despite dramatic increases in funding. In Sharpe's view, the economics of the illegal drug trade are such that even dramatic increases in drug seizures will have little impact on drug availability and use. Sharpe is a professor of political science at Swarthmore College and coauthor with Eva Bertram of *Drug War Politics: The Price of Denial*.

As you read, consider the following questions:

1. What has happened to the price of cocaine and heroin over the past fifteen years, as reported by the author?
2. According to the DEA official quoted by Sharpe, what percentage of their product could drug organizations lose to interdiction and still remain profitable?
3. How much cocaine is needed to supply all American users for a year, according to Sharpe?

The debate over drug interdiction long has been spiked with rhetoric and accusations. This year's [1996] election-year debate is no exception. Advocates for increased drug interdiction draw on compelling symbolic images: Without a strong interdiction program, they argue, we simply would be allowing this poison to flow across our borders and onto our city streets. But if public leaders are serious about alleviating drug use and abuse, they must abandon symbolic politics and take a cold, hard look at the logic and results of the interdiction campaigns into which U.S. officials already have poured billions of taxpayer dollars.

Neither candidate has been willing to take this step. Bob Dole backs a tougher interdiction effort. President Clinton, meanwhile, hardly is the anti-interdiction candidate Dole portrays. Congress already had cut the interdiction budget from $2 billion to $1.5 billion for fiscal 1993 when Clinton entered office in January. The White House backed a much smaller cut for fiscal 1994, based on internal studies demonstrating that "despite interdiction efforts . . . the availability of drugs has not been significantly reduced at home." This move drew a volley of attacks from drug warriors and, by 1996, the Clinton administration largely had reversed itself, pressing for a restoration of much of the 1993 cuts. In the end, Clinton has proved as reluctant as his Republican opponents to take on two fundamental questions: What is the record on drug interdiction and what are the prospects for success?

The drug warriors' faith in interdiction is based on a seemingly straightforward logic: Stop the cocaine and heroin being smuggled into our country before it crosses our borders. The more drugs interdicted, the less available—and that will drive up the street price of drugs and force down drug use. At one level, the logic is self-evident: The more we spend on Coast Guard and Navy patrols, as well as Customs inspections, the more drugs will be seized and the more traffickers arrested. Drug warriors carefully document the drop in drug seizures and arrests under Clinton and promise a big bang from the dollars they would have us spend.

BODY COUNTS

But these are the "body counts" in a losing battle against the drug supply. In fact, there is no evidence that increased drug interdiction has a meaningful effect on the price or even the overall availability of drugs. Clinton's critics blame the decline in heroin and cocaine prices since 1993—and increases in drug use—on Clinton's modest initial cuts in interdiction spending.

But they are silent about the fact that drug prices have been declining for the past 15 years—even during and after the drug wars of the eighties. Interdiction budgets increased from $350 million to $2 billion under Presidents Reagan and Bush—and street prices (in 1994 dollars) of a pure gram of cocaine plummeted from roughly $1,100 to about $175; a pure gram of heroin from about $3,800 to roughly $1,000.

Nor is there evidence that interdiction levels have had any lasting effect on the amount of drugs entering the United States—or available on our streets. Perhaps most importantly, drug warriors are unable to demonstrate the impact of interdiction on levels of use and abuse. They have been quick to show increases in emergency-room incidents involving heroin and cocaine since Clinton took office, but they say not a word about the dramatic worsening of hard-core drug abuse under Bush, despite his unprecedented interdiction campaigns. Cocaine-related hospital emergencies increased by 22 percent between 1988 and 1993, while heroin-related emergencies rose by 65 percent, more dramatic than the increase under Clinton.

A Lesson in Economics

The conclusion no candidate wants to admit is inescapable: Even the dramatic escalations in drug-law enforcement under Reagan and Bush (and, to be fair, under Clinton, who raised the enforcement budget 25 percent over Bush's last budget) are failing on their own terms—they are not making heroin and cocaine cheaper or less available, and they are not bringing down drug abuse and addiction. Understanding why increased interdiction never will have much effect on price is a lesson in Economics 101: The "enemy" we are fighting is not the drug producers, cartels or dealers. It is a market in economic goods under high demand.

Trying to suppress the drug trade through force is self-defeating for two reasons. First, cocaine and heroin are very cheap to grow, refine, ship and sell. The drug war tries to raise prices high enough to cut demand. It has managed to raise prices higher than they otherwise would be, but not high enough to keep drugs out of reach for most consumers. And raising prices also inflates profits: A pure gram of pharmaceutical cocaine that costs about $15, for example, brings about $150 on the black market. These high profits have a paradoxical effect: They provide a steady incentive for drug suppliers to remain in the trade and for new suppliers to enter. So the "stick" of law enforcement intended to discourage black marketeers simultaneously creates a "carrot"—enormous profits—which encourages them. As suppliers pursue these high profits, they keep the supply of drugs up and that keeps prices from increasing too much—undermining the aim of policy.

HITTING MERCURY

Thus, when shipments are seized, traffickers can draw on a cheap and almost unlimited supply of cocaine to pump into the pipeline, keeping up the supply entering the country. Production costs are so low and profits so extraordinary that "the average drug organization can afford to lose 70 percent to 80 percent of its product and still be profitable," explained one former Drug Enforcement Administration (DEA) official.

Second, cutting off trafficking routes is like cutting off the head of the mythical Greek Hydra: Multiple heads grow in its place. Cut one route and traffickers set up operations elsewhere to meet the profitable demand—thus shifting or even spreading coca production and distribution to new routes and regions. "It's like hitting mercury with a hammer," explained one State Department official.

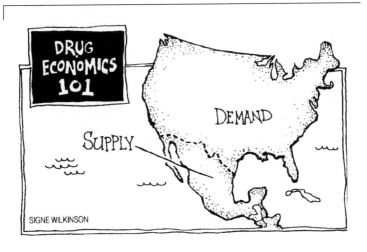

Signe Wilkinson/Cartoonists & Writers Syndicate. Reprinted by permission.

Look at the evidence. Drug-control campaigns against heroin in Turkey in the 1970s simply succeeded in stimulating heroin production in Southeast Asia, Afghanistan and Mexico. In the early 1980s, U.S. officials proudly pointed to the significant drop in cocaine smuggling after intense interdiction efforts in southern Florida. But before long, traffickers responded by shifting to air drops over the Caribbean Sea for pickup by boat. When enforcers caught up with this tactic, traffickers switched to new shipping routes through northern Mexico. Intensified enforcement there has led to a resurgence of trafficking in the Caribbean. When air routes are disrupted, traffickers switch to land-based routes. In every instance, the interdiction challenge is formidable: Analyst Mathea Falco argues that 13 trailer trucks can supply American cocaine consumption for one year; in 1994, 2.8 million trucks crossed our border from Mexico.

IMAGE OVER SUBSTANCE

Given these fatal flaws in the interdiction strategy, increased drug seizures and arrests are as meaningless as body counts—the numbers go up but so does the supply of drugs traffickers pump into new pipelines. That means that big interdiction budgets get us big seizures and big prison populations but little impact on drug prices or drug abuse. . . .

The conclusion is inescapable: Fighting an interdiction war against a drug market like this never will succeed in limiting supply or raising prices and availability enough to reduce use and abuse—no matter how much funding and firepower we invest or how effective our training and coordination are. Unfortunately, both sides in this campaign's great drug non-debate insist on image over substance—on appearing tough instead of acting smart. No elected official has the courage to say the emperor's drug war has no clothes—and then to launch a serious debate on how to reduce drug use and abuse.

"[Drug *Abuse Resistance Education*] in combination with follow-up and community wide initiatives may be found to dramatically lower drug use."

DRUG EDUCATION CAN REDUCE DRUG USE

Robert E. Peterson

School-based drug prevention programs have been criticized for failing to achieve their goal of reducing drug abuse. In the following viewpoint, Robert E. Peterson defends one such program—Drug Abuse Resistance Education (DARE)—against charges that it is ineffective. Peterson concedes that there is no evidence that DARE reduces drug use in the short term, but he insists that the program has many positive effects, including enhancing student awareness of the dangers of drug use and improving relations among students, police, and parents. Moreover, according to Peterson, research suggests that DARE and other school-based programs, when combined with community-wide prevention initiatives, can help reduce drug use among young people. Peterson, a former director of the Office of Drug Control Policy for the state of Michigan, is a lawyer in private practice in Oswego, New York.

As you read, consider the following questions:

1. According to Peterson, why are some parents opposed to DARE?
2. In the author's view, what is the weakness of the studies that find DARE ineffective at reducing drug use in the short term?
3. What is the most significant factor placing children at risk of drug use, according to Peterson?

Reprinted from Robert E. Peterson, "DARE Issues," a publication of the State of Michigan Office of Drug Control Policy, November 7, 1994, by permission of the author.

There are two main sources of criticism being leveled against DARE [Drug Abuse Resistance Education]. One raises legitimate issues that deserve attention regarding the effectiveness of the DARE program in reducing drug use among children. Ironically, the other source of criticism actually comes from drug using parents angry that DARE has made their children too anti-drug!

First, there is the legitimate concern that applies to all prevention programs being asked about whether the program is effective. There are sincere concerns regarding DARE program effectiveness and evaluation that require thoughtful review and response. The DARE program must remain open to continual revision, updating, and improvement. Key to this discussion is the definition of "effective" or "successful" and what standards are applied to measure this effect from any one program.

Second, there is an organized attack on DARE by well financed pro-drug legalization groups and even drug using parents who basically fear that the program has been too effective in making their children take an anti-drug stance. . . .

THE DRUG CULTURE'S ATTACK ON DARE

The nation's largest organization promoting drug legalization and drug law "reform" is the Drug Policy Foundation (DPF) in Washington, D.C. This group gave a $10,000 award to a defense attorney who was quoted as saying, "my sustenance is drugs and murder. . . . If you kill a cop, I'll pay to take the case," in an American Law News Service article by Michael Checcio. Loud applause and laughter greeted this lawyer and other speakers boasting of daily marijuana use at the 1992 DPF awards dinner.

The Drug Policy Foundation's Spring 1994 publication ran a story critical of DARE, citing negative evaluations and promising more in future editions. DPF board member and pro–drug reform advocate Nicholas Pastore, a police chief who reportedly dismantled his DARE program, is quoted in a High Times magazine article critical of DARE. Chief Pastore received a $10,000 award from the DPF. DPF also produced a show intended for public broadcasting regarding the "debate" about DARE. DPF recently received a $6 million commitment from a single donor.

The pro-marijuana smokers' magazine, High Times, has been more blatant in its attacks on DARE. Their June 1994 issue on DARE was called "Programming Fascism—The Drug War on Our Children" and included implications that DARE includes indoctrination, mind control, and turning children into "miniature drug warriors." The article includes a photograph and quotes from the founder of "Parents Against DARE," an organization founded when some drug using parents were being turned in by their children in the DARE program. A *Wall Street Journal* article states that the organization includes admitted pot smokers and quotes the organization's founder that DARE "is Big Brother putting spies in our homes."

EDUCATION DISCOURAGES ABUSE

To keep kids from starting on drugs requires the kind of education effort that has been used to discourage alcohol consumption. While it is not always 100 percent successful, continuous education about alcohol in schools, homes and churches has decreased the percentage of young kids drowning themselves in bottles of booze.

Robert A. Jordan, *San Diego North County Times*, March 18, 1997.

The primary basis for attacks on DARE by the drug culture is that drug using parents fear that DARE will cause their children to recognize, disapprove of, and perhaps report on their drug use. Their position appears to be that drug abuse in the home is to be kept a family secret and that drug use by adults in the home is acceptable. While organizations like "Parents Against DARE" state that they do not want their children to use drugs, they ignore the overwhelming evidence that parental drug use is the number one factor correlated with youth drug use.

DARE instructors do not allow students to name those who use drugs in the class, but students have come to DARE officers privately and asked to discuss drug use by parents and others. Schoolteachers and others who provide drug and child abuse prevention instruction often face a similar dilemma. Bringing drug and child abuse in the home to the attention of authorities is evidence of a program having a positive impact and can improve a child's odds of a healthy future. The key is having an effective intervention and response plan in place and to handle this information in a way that will ultimately benefit the child.

REPORTING PARENTAL DRUG USE

DARE opponents have used isolated incidences in which police responded to reported parental drug use and the child purportedly was upset by the police arrest and conviction of the parent. While drug using parents may conclude that it is better for children if parental drug use goes undetected, very few family counselors feel this way.

In the most celebrated case of a DARE student reporting on

her parents' drug use, reported in the *Wall Street Journal*, the mother who admitted to using pot was a school bus driver! The mother rightly concluded that "this would never have happened if we never smoked hemp." The parents also have vowed not to use illegal drugs again.

The fact that DARE has helped bring drug abuse in the home out of the closet is actually evidence of the program's effectiveness. To improve the program, police departments, treatment experts, and schools should coordinate and plan their response to drug use in the home. The best interests of the child should be the basis for the response agreed upon. Dealing with these situations is a sensitive and difficult task.

The possibility exists that isolated situations have occurred where the response could have been better coordinated. This certainly does not lead to the conclusion that DARE is at fault, or that drug abuse should remain a dirty little family secret.

REJECTING THE RIGHT TO USE DRUGS

A number of those in the pro-drug movement maintain that drug use in the home is an individual right and have outdated views on the dangers of illegal drugs, especially marijuana. They fear the anti-drug information in DARE and "wonder if the minds of their DARE children are being poisoned against them."

The founder of Parents Against DARE challenges the marijuana information provided by a DARE officer as being incorrect and contradicts it with a text authored by one of the National Organization for Marijuana Reform's (NORML) most recent board members. NORML is the nation's oldest marijuana smokers' lobby. It was founded with a grant from *Playboy* in the early 1970's and its founder once stated that he favored drug legalization with no age limits on drug access.

In an appearance with NORML's current director (who admits to regular pot use) and other drug legalization advocates celebrating the 50th anniversary of LSD, Marsha Rosenbaum of the National Council on Crime and Delinquency expressed her fear that drug education programs were turning her "children into loyal soldiers in the war on drugs" and making her a "liar" in her own home. John Morgan, a new NORML board member, agreed with her statement that "I would go with the notion that drugs are a private kind of enterprise, if you will, and that we ought to leave it out of schools." To some opposed to DARE, the best drug education is no drug education at all.

Ironically, some who fear that DARE is making their child too anti-drug also try to align with conservative groups who fear that DARE is too liberal in its approach and exposes children to nondirective and open ended teachings. In fact, while Parents Against DARE criticizes DARE for "putting spies in our homes" and making kids so anti-drug that they turn in their parents, this same group also complains that DARE does not tell kids not to use drugs outright and fails to judge drug use as wrong and harmful. . . .

EVALUATING THE SUCCESS OF DARE

There is a legitimate question lingering on whether DARE, or for that matter any prevention program, actually works. Social scientists agree that finding the answer to this question is not an easy task. Over the years, can one attribute drug use or nonuse behavior to any one program? . . .

Unfortunately, research on DARE often does not explore the broader effect of DARE, but limits inquiry into whether DARE alone prevents kids from using drugs. It is a valid question. DARE does promote itself as "keeping kids off drugs." But it is a limiting question, and DARE's impact on "keeping kids off drugs" should be explored in a far more comprehensive school and community prevention context.

MANY POSITIVE EFFECTS

Research on DARE's effectiveness has produced mixed results. DARE has been reviewed and evaluated more than any other prevention program. A synopsis of over 18 evaluations of DARE reveals that DARE consistently has many positive effects, such as:

- DARE builds bridges among students, law enforcement, educators, parents, and the business community. Study after study attests that DARE is supported and appreciated by students, parents, teachers, and police agencies. Process evaluations demonstrate the program is effectively and professionally implemented.
- DARE increases student and parent confidence that they can avoid drugs and deal with peer pressure.
- DARE enhances public awareness of substance abuse issues and prevention education.
- DARE increases student knowledge of the nature and consequences of drug use.
- DARE builds positive student attitudes.
- DARE builds strong social norms and understanding of advertising influences.
- DARE improves student attitudes toward law enforcement.
- DARE impacts on some of the precedents to drug use.

However, according to recent research, DARE has not been shown to consistently lower drug use over the short term. This research conclusion has numerous weaknesses. One problem is that drug use is so low among younger children that the proportionate changes in use for DARE and non-DARE students is negligible. Even if the short term drug use impact is unproven, does that negate possible longer term effects? Also, the question of what impact DARE has when it is part of a comprehensive continuum of drug prevention intervention has never been addressed.

A deeper issue remains, even if it is shown that a single fifth or sixth grade DARE classroom program *alone* does not reduce drug use over a few years, does it lead to the conclusion that the program is ineffective?

DOES DARE REDUCE DRUG USE?

It is important at the outset to note that no drug prevention program working in isolation has been proven to prevent drug use among youth over the long run. One year of DARE does not provide a lifetime inoculation against drug use and it should not be expected to do so. If a magic bullet existed to prevent drug use, we would not have a drug problem today.

A recent major evaluation of DARE that reviewed and combined the results of eight previous DARE studies concluded that DARE did not impact on student alcohol or marijuana use rates. The study found that DARE did reduce tobacco use and it did not review the use of cocaine, LSD, or other drugs. The study also concluded that DARE was not as effective as other more interactive prevention programs. This federally funded evaluation by the Research Triangle Institute has created a storm of media reporting and controversy.

The National Institute of Justice did not publish the report because of its failure to meet standards of its peer review panel. The *American Journal of Public Health* did publish the study after review by its experts. Media reports alleged that the study was being suppressed by the federal government, but it is available from the Justice Department upon request.

The study did find that DARE resulted in improved student knowledge of drug dangers and consequences; increased student social skills; better student attitudes toward police; stronger attitudes against drug use; and enhanced self-esteem. These positive changes have generally been ignored in media reports. . . .

Comparing DARE to other prevention approaches, the study noted that the impact of DARE was greater than non-interactive drug programs, but less than that of more interactive prevention programs. The authors noted the general failure of affective education approaches and noted that recent modifications to the core DARE curriculum "may lead to greater program effectiveness."

The authors further noted that DARE's cumulative effects, where DARE is continued in later grades, may be greater and that the impact on community wide initiatives was not measured. Harvard lecturer and study review panelist William De-Jong cautioned that the programs DARE was compared with may not have been appropriate.

The weight and implications of this study are yet to be determined. It certainly has serious limitations and there is a potential for various interest groups to use it to promote an anti-DARE agenda. The study may also be viewed as providing some interesting insight and opening up a range of issues worthy of further exploration.

Even drug prevention programs that are presented in every grade and integrated with other curriculum failed to impact on drug use unless the program was part of a community wide consistent prevention effort. In Kansas City, a drug prevention program was taught in two contexts. One group of students received the drug prevention program in school classrooms only and another was exposed to the program together with community wide prevention initiatives. Drug use among the school classroom only group was not affected, but when the program was part of a community wide effort, significantly lower drug use was demonstrated.

Research shows that the effects of any education program diminish over time and must be reinforced. The DARE researchers stated that DARE's middle school follow-up curriculum may make DARE more effective. Drug prevention must be reinforced in the home, in the community, and among peers—not just in the classroom. Many factors impact on student drug use. For example, the number one correlated factor that places children at risk of drug use is use by their parents. Drug using parents oppose DARE because the program has brought parental use into the light. Parents who use drugs are likely to reverse DARE's message and impact among their children.

DARE evaluations consistently fail to consider DARE in the context of broader prevention initiatives and follow-up. Research has focused on whether exposure to DARE alone in either fifth or sixth grade leads to lower drug use over time. Instead, DARE should be viewed as an important piece of the drug prevention puzzle that in combination with follow-up and community wide initiatives may be found to dramatically lower drug use.

> "Clearly the impact [of drug-education programs] is negligible. Indeed, federal spending on drug-education programs and activities might have made things worse."

DRUG EDUCATION MAY ENCOURAGE DRUG USE

D.M. Gorman

Many people, including government officials and members of the media, believe that drug-education programs ought to be a priority in the current war on drugs. In the following viewpoint, D.M. Gorman challenges the conventional thinking on this topic, arguing that there is no evidence that drug education has succeeded in reducing drug abuse. To the contrary, Gorman contends that drug-education programs may actually have contributed to drug abuse in various ways. Gorman is the director of prevention research at the Center of Alcohol Studies and an assistant professor in urban studies at Rutgers University.

As you read, consider the following questions:

1. According to Gorman, what does the recent increase in teenage use of marijuana demonstrate about increased federal drug-education spending?
2. In the author's opinion, why is the "social skills" approach to drug education inapplicable to most teenage drug users?
3. How successful has the Life Skills Training program been, in Gorman's view?

Excerpted from D.M. Gorman, "The Failure of Drug Education," Public Interest, no. 129, Fall 1997, pp. 50–60. Reprinted with the permission of the author and the Public Interest; ©1997 by National Affairs, Inc.

The role of the federal government in preventing adolescent drug use was a central issue of the 1996 presidential campaign. Bob Dole criticized the Clinton administration for slashing the staff of the Office of National Drug Control Policy (ONDCP) while Clinton criticized attempts by the Republican majority in Congress to cut federal support of drug-prevention programs—the most dramatic being a proposal to rescind the entire $482 million prevention budget of the Department of Education. It seemed as though everyone, Democrats and Republicans, liberals and conservatives, wanted to be seen as favoring federal spending on drug prevention and, in particular, drug education.

Indeed, 65 percent of congressional candidates polled in 1996 by the Community Anti-Drug Coalitions of America ranked prevention programs as the number one priority in reducing the country's drug problem, compared to just 9 percent for both interdiction and treatment. By the close of 1996, Republicans had abandoned their attempts to reduce the federal prevention budget and Clinton had secured extra funds for drug-education programs within the Department of Health and Human Services and the Department of Education.

There is no mystery in the bipartisan popularity of such education programs. Recently completed large-scale surveys have shown that illicit drug use among young people (primarily in the form of marijuana smoking) increased between 1992 and 1995, following more than a decade of steady decline. In the *National Household Survey*, conducted by the Department of Health and Human Services, monthly marijuana use among children between 12 and 17 increased from 4 percent in 1992 to more than 7 percent in 1994 while the perceived risks of use declined. The National Institute on Drug Abuse's *Monitoring the Future Study* showed that this trend was evident among eighth, tenth, and twelfth graders. Among the latter, reported use of any illicit drug during the previous 30 days rose from 14.4 percent in 1992 to 23.8 percent in 1995.

A LAUDABLE ENTERPRISE?

Advocates of drug education, from Health and Human Services Secretary Donna Shalala to former drug czar William Bennett, argue that federally funded initiatives of the past 10 years contributed, at least in part, to the decline in adolescent drug taking, and that cuts in federal spending led to the recent increased use. However, unlike other aspects of drug-control policy, prevention or education has been hardly analyzed. Law enforcement and interdiction efforts have been the subject of debate in both the popular press and academic circles, as have such treatments as needle exchange and methadone maintenance. In contrast, prevention is simply assumed to be a laudable enterprise, and, as will be discussed later, the claims of its proponents are uncritically accepted by the press and policy makers. But is it really the case that such programs succeed? And, more particularly, did federal spending on drug-prevention activities play a role in reducing adolescent drug use over the past 10 years? . . .

Data contained in the National Institute on Drug Abuse's *Monitoring the Future Study*—the main source for tracking adolescent drug use—and ONDCP's *National Drug Control Strategy*—the primary source for identifying federal expenditures across agencies and functions—enable one to assess the relationship between annual federal expenditures on drug-use prevention and the prevalence of illicit drug use among adolescents. . . .

DECLINING DRUG USE

Examination of data contained in the two documents reveals drug use was falling steadily among young people prior to the increase in government spending that occurred in the late 1980s. By 1987, when federal spending really began to accelerate, the proportion of twelfth graders reporting use of any illicit substance had already fallen to 25 percent, from its high of 39 percent in 1979. The figure was down to 17 percent when the federal drug-prevention budget crossed the billion-dollar threshold in 1990. Between 1981 and 1992, 30-day prevalence of illicit drug use fell by three-fifths (from 36.9 percent to 14.4 percent). The rate of decline was virtually the same during years of modest federal spending (1981–1986), as during years of accelerated federal spending (1987–1991). During the former period, the average yearly growth in the drug-prevention budget was $11.5 million, with a corresponding average yearly decline in drug use of 1.7 percent. During the latter period, there was close to a 25-fold increase in the size of the average yearly growth of the prevention budget ($281 million per annum), while the average decline in drug use rose by just one-half of 1 percent per year (to 2.2 percent).

Federal budgets, of course, represent less than half of what the nation spends on policies to reduce illicit drug use, even following the huge post-1986 increase. And the level of drug use is influenced by numerous factors other than federally funded initiatives. However, the above statistics are sufficient to address the fundamental issue raised by advocates of current drug-prevention policies and programs—namely, whether a sustained level of federal funding is necessary to reduce drug use among young people. Clearly the impact is negligible. Indeed, federal spending on drug-education programs and activities might have made things worse.

LAG TIME

At first glance, this admittedly seems unlikely. The federal budget began to increase five years before the rise in reported drug use. However, it is important to note that the agency budgets listed in the *National Drug Control Strategy* refer to federal appropriations, not actual spending on programmatic activity. These appropriations typically take time to filter down to the state and local level—for example, most of the Drug-Free Schools and Community funds authorized by the 1986 Anti-Drug Abuse Act were not available to local education agencies until early 1988. These agencies had then to recruit staff and to select curricula, before actually implementing their programs. Moreover, the effects of these activities on recipients' drug use would not be evident for some time, perhaps a year or two. Given this, it seems reasonable to assume that there is a lag of three to five years between the appropriation of moneys for drug-prevention programs and the manifestation of their effects on rates of adolescent drug use. Accordingly, the period of rapid federal spending, which commenced in 1987, coincides—closely in the case of a three-year lag, or exactly in the case of a five-year lag—to the period of increased drug use (1992 to 1995).

EVALUATING DRUG-EDUCATION PROGRAMS

How might federal spending on drug prevention have encouraged drug use? This is a difficult question to answer, as details on exactly how the money is spent are sparse and controlled studies of programs rare. However, an examination of school-based-prevention programs—the mainstay of drug prevention in the United States—suggests why drug-prevention activities might have unintended consequences.

Prior to the mid-1980s, there existed little or no research indicating that school-based prevention was an effective means of reducing drug use among young people. Indeed, many researchers believed that such education could do as much harm as good. . . .

Opinions differed regarding why prevention efforts could produce increased drug use. Some blamed the content of the programs: Knowledge-based programs of the 1960s and 1970s simply piqued students interest while the values-clarification methods of the mid-1970s confused students in that they failed to condemn drug use unambiguously. But others argued that it was the "zero tolerance" message that was at fault, insofar as it inspired incredulity and skepticism among many young people.

A THUNDERING BUST

The massively funded DARE program has been a thundering bust. That was the conclusion of a review of 120 separate studies of DARE paid for by the Department of Justice in 1994 but never published. In California, a comprehensive study commissioned by the state Department of Education also was suppressed because it came to the same conclusion: Ideological rigidity and effective education do not mix.

Robert Scheer, *Los Angeles Times*, December 31, 1996.

Despite these doubts, by the end of the 1980s, the prevailing wisdom among researchers, educators, and policy makers was that school-based programs could prevent adolescents from using drugs, providing the right type of program was used. And a growing body of empirical evidence, it was argued, demonstrated the effectiveness of a new type of curriculum, based on the principles of social-learning theory, the so-called "social-influence" approach.

SOCIAL SKILLS TRAINING

Social-influence programs retained the zero-tolerance message of their predecessors—all drug use was considered harmful and wrong. In addition, however, students were now taught the social skills that were supposedly necessary to remain drug free: In some cases, the programs employed a narrowly focused approach primarily concerned with teaching drug-resistance skills; in others, a broad-based approach was used to enhance a wide range of "life skills." The former type of program, called "resistance-skills training," could be delivered in eight to 10 classroom sessions. The latter, called "social-skills training," took 15 to 20 sessions to deliver. The latter are now more popular, at least among academics and policy makers. (The technique has been applied to problem behaviors other than drug use; for example, violence and teen sex.)

The programs attempt to teach "affective techniques," such as assertiveness training, self-esteem enhancement, and improved decision making. A person who possesses these skills, it is argued, is better able to cope with life and, hence, has no reason to experiment with drugs. In short, the underlying assumption is that young people who use drugs are socially incompetent. But there is little empirical evidence to support this idea. A study by Jonathan Shedler and Jack Block, researchers from the University of California at Berkeley, in the 1990 *American Psychologist*, for example, found that adolescents who engaged in experimental drug use were psychologically *better* adjusted than either heavy users or abstainers. Needless to say, this study is seldom cited by prevention advocates. . . .

LIMITATIONS OF LIFE SKILLS TRAINING

Some researchers will now admit that drug-education programs do not work. They are especially willing to criticize the widely adopted DARE [Drug Abuse Resistance Education] program. But they are quick to add that the problem is not drug education but the type of program adopted. What is needed is more federal money on "state-of-the-art" programs.

The state-of-the-art program most frequently mentioned in the popular press, as well as in academic journals, is the Life Skills Training (LST) program of Gilbert Botvin. Both the *New York Times* and *Time* recently carried pieces that contrasted the research records of DARE and LST. The largest longitudinal evaluation of the LST program, the *New York Times* noted, showed that

> behavioral changes initiated by the program lasted the entire six years of the study. The use of cigarettes, alcohol and marijuana among teenagers who had had the program was *half that of similar teen-agers who had not had the program* [emphasis added].

Both the *New York Times* and *Time* concluded that what was needed was for the LST program to be marketed and disseminated with the skill and aggression used for DARE.

The study referred to in both of these articles is a six-year follow-up of about 3,500 adolescents reported in the *Journal of the American Medical Association* in 1995. Once again, however, careful examination shows that the claims being made on behalf of the program are largely unsupported by the data presented in the article. Among all subjects for whom follow-up data were available, there were no statistically significant differences in illicit drug use between those who received the program and those who did not. Thirteen percent of LST subjects reported monthly marijuana use compared to 14 percent of control subjects; weekly use was 6 percent and 9 percent, respectively. How then does the *New York Times* report reductions of 50 percent in marijuana use?

The answer lies in the fact that the study presents an additional set of analyses based on a so-called "high fidelity" sample. To be included in this group, an individual had to receive at least 60 percent of the intervention over the three-year period during which it was delivered. . . . A comparison of this refined sample of program recipients with the control subjects produced statistically significant differences. . . .

As far as one can determine from the published data, the high-fidelity group represents less than half of those recruited into the intervention at the start of the project. It is a self-selected sub-sample that is no longer comparable to subjects in the control group. There are probably many drug-control activities that would appear to be effective under conditions where those who did not receive some ideal "dosage" of intervention are discounted. . . .

Unfortunately, the weaknesses of the LST programs are common in the field of drug prevention. Another key issue here is the almost total absence of independent evaluation: With very few exceptions, programs are developed, implemented, evaluated, and marketed by the same group of people. Much of the research in this area has a decidedly inductive quality—its goal being to prove that the program under study is effective.

Limited Expertise

Despite claims to the contrary, available data do not support the view that the decline in adolescent drug use that occurred between the early 1980s and early 1990s was influenced by the level of federal spending on drug-education activities. Indeed, if one takes into account the fact that the effects of spending do not manifest themselves in actual behavior for at least three years, then increased spending coincided with increased drug use.

The massive increase in federal spending that occurred in the mid-1980s drew a lot of people and programs into the drug-prevention arena in an indiscriminate manner. Politicians apparently believed that there existed sufficient latent skills and expertise to put these moneys to good use—that there were school superintendents, principals, teachers, community activists, local government officials, and others who knew what effective drug prevention was and how to deliver it efficiently to those most in need. They appear to have been mistaken. A good deal of this money went to people with limited experience and expertise in drug prevention. It is thus hardly surprising that we often get more, not less, drug use as a result of these activities.

Moreover, nobody really knows what an effective drug-education program would look like. In the mid-1980s, when the federal government began to embrace the social-influence model, there was little evidence that it could reduce drug use. Recent evaluations show that programs that purport to be effective in reducing adolescent experimentation with drugs, do so only when highly self-selected sub-samples are used in data analysis. Contrary to what is now being said in the popular press, these programs are unlikely to have any significant effect on adolescent drug use. There never was, and nor is there now, strong empirical evidence to show that social-influence programs can succeed where previous forms of drug-prevention activities failed.

More Harm than Good?

Where does this leave us? First of all, it is imperative that we avoid the temptation to make lavish claims about other ways of dealing with teenage drug use (e.g., law enforcement, interdiction, or "decriminalization"), simply because the evidence concerning drug prevention is so weak. We need to be guided by evidence concerning the effects of a particular approach on drug use, not by what we hope its effects will be or by the assumed good intentions of those who develop and implement programmatic activities.

With regard to education, the available evidence indicates that we have yet to develop strategies that can significantly reduce illicit drug use among young people. We could almost certainly stop funding certain activities, such as school-based prevention programs, with no adverse consequences. However, given the bipartisan popularity of drug education, dramatic reductions in federal drug-prevention funding are unlikely to occur, at least in the near future. In the meantime, local agencies such as school boards and city councils need to establish exactly what their drug-prevention dollars are buying. They should cease funding activities that have the potential to do harm and ensure that claims concerning new, more effective programs are subject to assessment by independent observers. Until that is done no one will know whether education efforts are doing more harm than good.

PERIODICAL BIBLIOGRAPHY

The following articles have been selected to supplement the diverse views presented in this chapter. Addresses are provided for periodicals not indexed in the *Readers' Guide to Periodical Literature*, the *Alternative Press Index*, the *Social Sciences Index*, or the *Index to Legal Periodicals and Books*.

William J. Bennett and John P. Walters	"Drugs: Face the Facts, Focus on Education," *Insight*, March 6, 1995. Available from 3600 New York Ave. NE, Washington, DC 20002.
Eva Bertram and Kenneth Sharpe	"The Drug War's Phony Fix: Why Certification Doesn't Work," *Nation*, April 28, 1997.
James Bovard	"Unsafe at Any Speed," *American Spectator*, April 1996.
Stephen Glass	"Don't You D.A.R.E.," *New Republic*, March 3, 1997.
Elizabeth Guia and Oscar Padilla	"Fighting Drugs at the Source," *World & I*, November 1996. Available from 3600 New York Ave. NE, Washington, DC 20002.
Alfred McCoy	"Drug Fallout," *Progressive*, August 1997.
Ethan Nadelmann and Jennifer McNeely	"Doing Methadone Right," *Public Interest*, Spring 1996.
William O'Brien, interview by George M. Anderson.	"The Crisis in Drug Treatment: An Interview with William O'Brien," *America*, March 16, 1996.
Phyllis Schlafly	"The Scandal of What Is Called Drug Education," *Conservative Chronicle*, September 18, 1996. Available from PO Box 11297, Des Moines, IA 50340-1297.
David Van Biema	"Just Say Life Skills: A New School Antidrug Program Outstrips D.A.R.E.," *Time*, November 11, 1996.
Christopher S. Wren	"Why Seizing Drugs Barely Dents Supply," *New York Times*, December 15, 1996.
Coletta Youngers	"The Only War We've Got: Drug Enforcement in Latin America," *NACLA Report on the Americas*, September/October 1997.

CHAPTER 3

IS LEGALIZATION A REALISTIC ALTERNATIVE TO THE WAR ON DRUGS?

CHAPTER PREFACE

In February 1996, the conservative journal *National Review* published a special issue in which several writers declared the war on drugs a failure and advocated some form of drug legalization as a solution to the problems created by illegal drugs. The collective position of these writers was summed up by editor William F. Buckley Jr., who concluded that the war on drugs "is wasting our resources, and it is encouraging civil, judicial and penal procedures associated with police states. We all agree on movement toward legalization."

Advocates of legalization contend that legalizing drugs would benefit society in many ways. Legalization, they believe, would result in a massive decrease in crime rates because it would end the corruption and violent turf wars associated with the underground market for drugs. It would reduce the prison population by 50 percent, proponents maintain, and it would cut the caseload of an overburdened legal system by half. Advocates also insist that legalization would free up the billions of dollars currently being spent on the war on drugs, which could then be spent on drug education, on the treatment of hard-core addicts, and on law enforcement efforts against serious crime. Proponents also insist that legalization would introduce standards concerning drug purity and dosage that would lower the incidence of drug-related deaths.

Critics of the legalization position counter that the immediate result of such a move would be to increase the number of casual drug users dramatically, which would in turn increase the number of drug abusers and addicts. This would lead to increases in crimes induced by drug taking, in health problems, and in death rates among users. "Health and productivity costs would increase dramatically, and . . . the human costs from drug use would rise over time as more people who tried the drugs used them and became addicted," argues Georgetown University professor Robert L. DuPont. According to critics, while some crime rates would go down and prisons and courts would benefit from legalization, the increase in health costs and in drug-induced crimes would make legalization a losing proposition.

The viewpoints in the following chapter debate the probable costs and benefits of the proposed policy of legalizing drugs in the United States.

| "Scrap the nonsense of trying to obliterate drugs and acknowledge their presence in our society as we have with alcohol and tobacco."

THE LEGALIZATION OF DRUGS WOULD BENEFIT SOCIETY

Benson B. Roe

In the following viewpoint, Benson B. Roe contends that since illegal drugs cannot be eradicated from society, and since such drugs are no more harmful than many legal substances, most illegal drugs should be legalized. As a heart surgeon, Roe has seen the harmful effects that drugs can have on the human body, yet he believes that illegal drugs are not the evil, addictive, and poisonous substances many people claim they are. The benefits of legalization, according to Roe, would include drug purity assurance, reduction of drug crime, savings in law enforcement costs, and new tax revenues. Roe is professor emeritus and former chair of cardiothoracic surgery at the University of California at San Francisco.

As you read, consider the following questions:
1. What is wrong with using the term "addiction" to describe most drug use, according to the author?
2. In Roe's view, what kind of people must a large proportion of drug users be?
3. Why does Roe think that legalization of drugs in the near future is highly unlikely?

Reprinted from Benson B. Roe, "Why We Should Legalize Drugs," on-line article at www.calyx.net/~schaffer/MISC/roe1.html, June 2, 1997, by permission of the author.

More than 20 years ago when I was removing destroyed heart valves from infected intravenous drug abusers I assumed that these seriously ill patients represented just the tip of the iceberg of narcotic abuse. In an effort to ascertain what proportion of serious or fatal drug-related disease this group represented, I sought information from the San Francisco Coroner. To my surprise he reported that infections from contaminated intravenous injections were the only cause of drug-related deaths he saw except for occasional deaths from overdoses. He confirmed the inference that clean, reasonable dosages of heroin, cocaine and marijuana are pathologically harmless. He asserted he had never seen a heroin user over the age of 50. My obvious conclusion was that they had died from their habit but he was confident that they had simply tired of the drug and just quit. When asked if the same were basically true of marijuana and cocaine, he responded affirmatively. That caused me to wonder why these substances had been made illegal.

It is frequently stated that illicit drugs are "bad, dangerous, destructive" or "addictive," and that society has an obligation to keep them from the public. But nowhere can be found reliable, objective scientific evidence that they are any more harmful than other substances and activities that are legal. In view of the enormous expense, the carnage and the obvious futility of the "drug war," resulting in massive criminalization of society, it is high time to examine the supposed justification for keeping certain substances illegal. Those who initiated those prohibitions and those who now so vigorously seek to enforce them have not made their objectives clear. Are they to protect us from evil, from addiction, or from poison?

EVIL, ADDICTIVE, AND POISONOUS

The concept of evil is derived from subjective values and is difficult to define. Just why certain (illegal) substances are singularly more evil than legal substances like alcohol has not been explained. This complex subject of "right" and "wrong" has never been successfully addressed by legislation and is best left to the pulpit.

Addiction is also a relative and ubiquitous phenomenon. It certainly cannot be applied only to a short arbitrary list of addictive substances while ignoring a plethora of human cravings—from chocolate to coffee, from gum to gambling, from tea to tobacco, from snuggling to sex. Compulsive urges to fulfill a perceived need are ubiquitous. Some people are more susceptible to addiction than others and some "needs" are more addictive than others. Probably the most addictive substance in our civilization is tobacco—yet no one has suggested making it illegal.

As for prohibition, it has been clearly demonstrated that when an addictive desire becomes inaccessible it provokes irresponsible behavior to fulfill that desire. Education and support at least have a chance of controlling addiction. Deprivation only sharpens the craving and never works. Even in prison addicts are able to get their "fix."

A REGULATORY ALTERNATIVE IS NEEDED

Drug legalization, a euphemism for ending drug prohibition and the so-called War on Drugs, is a provocative idea. Its supporters have an overwhelming wealth of evidence to describe just how destructive current drug policies have been to our criminal justice system, our cities and our country. Yet legalization's advocates have been losing the public debate because they have failed to propose a sensible regulatory alternative to prohibition. With the issue framed today as legalization versus war, war easily prevails. Americans like the idea of a war against something evil. . . .

The advocates of a drug war will prevail, so long as supporters of legalization fail to propose an alternative defining exactly how government might regulate the sale and distribution of drugs.

Theodore W. Kheel, *City Limits*, November 1995.

And "poison" is also a misleading shibboleth. The widespread propaganda that illegal drugs are "deadly poisons" is a hoax. There is little or no medical evidence of long term ill effects from sustained, moderate consumption of uncontaminated marijuana, cocaine or heroin. If these substances—most of them have been consumed in large quantities for centuries—were responsible for any chronic, progressive or disabling diseases, they certainly would have shown up in clinical practice and/or on the autopsy table. But they simply have not!

CONVENTIONAL LIVES

Media focus on the "junkie" has generated a mistaken impression that all uses of illegal drugs are devastated by their habit. Simple arithmetic demonstrates that the small population of visible addicts must constitute only a fraction of the $150 billion per year illegal drug market. This industry is so huge that it necessarily encompasses a very large portion of the ordinary population who are typically employed, productive, responsible and not significantly impaired from leading conventional lives. These drug users are not "addicts" just as the vast majority of alcohol users are not "alcoholics."

Is it not a ridiculous paradox to have laws to protect us from relatively harmless substances and not from the devastating effects of other substances that happen to be legal? It is well known that tobacco causes nearly a million deaths annually (in the US alone) from cancer, cardiovascular disease and emphysema; more than 350,000 die from alcohol-related cirrhosis and its complications; and caffeine is the cause of cardiac and nervous system disturbances. These facts suggest that the public is being fraudulently misled into fearing the wrong substances and into complacency about hazardous substances by allowing their sale and even subsidization.

Our environment contains a plethora of hazards, of which recreational substances are much less important than many others. Recognizing the reality of consumer demand and the perspective of relative harm should make a strong case for alternatives to prohibition. Should we not have learned from the failure of the Volstead Act of the 1920s and the current ubiquitous availability of illegal drugs that prohibition is the height of futility?

THE LEGALIZATION ALTERNATIVE

Is it not time to recognize that the "problem" is not the drugs but the enormous amounts of untaxed money diverted from the economy to criminals? The economic incentive for drug dealers to merchandise their product aggressively is a multi-billion dollar return which has a far more powerful effect to increase substance abuse than any enforcement program can possibly do to constrain that usage. The hopeless challenge of drug crime is compounded by the parallel expansion of theft crime, which is the principal economic resource to finance the drug industry. How can this be anything but a lose-lose situation for society?

We should look at the fact that a relatively low budget public education campaign has resulted in a significant decline in US consumption of both alcohol and tobacco during a period when a costly and intensive campaign to curtail illegal drugs only resulted in their increased usage. Is there a lesson to be heeded?

Of course there is. Scrap the nonsense of trying to obliterate drugs and acknowledge their presence in our society as we have with alcohol and tobacco. Legalization would result in:

1. purity assurance under Food and Drug Administration regulation;

2. labeled concentration of the product (to avoid overdose);
3. obliteration of vigorous marketing ("pushers");
4. obliteration of drug crime and reduction of theft crime;
5. savings in expensive enforcement; and
6. significant tax revenues.

Effort and funds can then be directed to educating the public about the hazards of all drugs.

Can such a change of attitude happen? Probably not, because the huge illegal drug industry has mountains of money for a media blitz and for buying politicians to sing the songs of "evil" and "danger" which is certain to kill any legislative attempt at legalization. Perhaps it will take some time before reality can prevail, but meanwhile we should at least do more to expose deception and to disseminate the truth.

"*As psychotropic drug use increased after legalization, the death toll and collateral costs also would rise. Legalization arguments ignore this.*"

THE LEGALIZATION OF DRUGS WOULD BE HARMFUL TO SOCIETY

William J. Olson

In the following viewpoint, William J. Olson argues that advocates of drug legalization make too many optimistic assumptions about the impact of their proposal. In contrast to proponents of legalization, Olson contends that drugs create significant health problems and that use and abuse of drugs would definitely increase under legalization, resulting in an increase in the nation's health care costs. Olson, formerly a deputy assistant at the Department of State, is a senior fellow at the National Strategy Information Center, a Washington, D.C., public policy think tank.

As you read, consider the following questions:
1. How does Olson refute the argument that the use of drugs is no more hazardous than other risky behaviors, such as dangerous sports?
2. According to the author, how does the Swiss experiment illustrate what would happen under legalization?
3. In Olson's view, why is it illogical to argue that because tobacco and alcohol are legal, drugs should also be legal?

Reprinted from William J. Olson, "Why Americans Should Resist the Legalization of Drugs," *Backgrounder*, July 18, 1994, by permission of the Heritage Foundation, Washington, D.C.

Some advocates of legalization contend that the dangers of drug use are overstated and do not warrant strong enforcement efforts. Taken literally, this argument was more plausible in the 1960s and 1970s, when less was known about the full effects of many drugs. Few now claim that the use of psychotropic drugs represents no serious health hazard and that use should be celebrated as a liberation of consciousness. Instead, the most visible spokesmen for this view, such as Professor Ethan Nadelmann of the Woodrow Wilson School, assert that such drug use represents no special liability, certainly none greater than tobacco or alcohol, that justifies prohibition. "The logic of legalization," says Nadelmann, "depends in part upon two assumptions: that most illegal drugs are not as dangerous as is commonly believed, and that the most risky of them are unlikely to prove widely appealing precisely because of the obvious danger."

This is not an isolated view. Steven Duke and Albert Gross, in their book *America's Longest War: Rethinking Our Tragic Crusade Against Drugs*, with an introduction by Baltimore mayor Kurt Schmoke, offer the observation that "the risks of psychoactive drug use are substantial but no greater than those accompanying many other recreational activities" such as hang-gliding, boxing, mountain climbing, motorcycle riding, hunting, bicycle riding, or boating. Echoing Nadelmann, they argue that "the use of heroin and cocaine in a free market system would adversely affect the quality of the lives of the users and those around them in a way not appreciably different than does alcohol use" and that "the total number of drug abusers . . . would not be essentially different than is the case in our hybrid system of legalization." Or, "Hardly anyone would be a drug abuser who does not already abuse at least one psychoactive drug."

RISKY BEHAVIOR

For this to be true, for the same number of people engaged in these other "risky" activities as in using drugs, one would expect to see a corresponding number of lives cut short and other consequences. Thus, one would have to expect that some loss of life, increased health care costs, lost labor, family violence, higher crime, damaged fetuses, and so forth be counted among the costs of recreational biking, boxing, hunting, sports, gardening, and similarly risky behaviors. For example, drug-using workers are 3 to 4 times as likely to have on-the-job accidents, 4 to 6 times more likely to have off-the-job accidents, 2 to 3 times more likely to file medical claims, 5 times more likely to file workman's compensation, and 25 percent to 35 percent less productive on the job. Yet nobody suggests that bicycling addicts and others impose corresponding broad-ranging increases in personal costs that the whole community must bear.

Americans are not living in the 1970s, or the age of *Reefer Madness*, when there was little scientific research on the addictive nature of psychotropic drugs or the considerable health consequences of prolonged exposure to them. Quite the contrary. Recent medical evidence on the effects of drug use has forced supporters of legalization to stress the need for sustained, vigorous treatment programs—a frank admission that there is a serious health hazard. But they still downplay the dangerous aspects of drug use. Even if this hazard were no greater than that represented by tobacco (a generous concession) there would be no comfort in recapitulating the catastrophe of widespread tobacco use.

Anti-Drug Laws Have Merit

If society views the human body as merely a more complicated evolutionary product than a cabbage, then by all means, let's dispense with anti-drug laws and save money for those of us who are not addicted, who have no interest in drugs and who would like to take nighttime walks through our cities. But if our bodies are "temples of God," and if laws are for the purpose of restricting behavior that damages the temples of those who are not constrained by a higher power, then anti-drug laws have merit.

Cal Thomas, *Conservative Chronicle*, February 14, 1996.

Tobacco is implicated directly in some 300,000 premature deaths in the United States each year. The immense collateral costs in health care requirements, lost labor, damaged fetuses, and debilitated lives run to billions of dollars. Reliable figures place drug-related premature deaths, at current levels of use, at somewhere between 3,000 and 20,000, added to which are the correspondingly high collateral costs. An intuitive argument would hold that as psychotropic drug use increased after legalization, the death toll and collateral costs also would rise. Legalization arguments ignore this. But what of the second assumption: that legalization would not result in dramatic increases in the use of these drugs precisely because they are so dangerous?

International Experience

The contention that legalization would not trigger large increases in use is based on optimism rather than evidence. Of course, the contention cannot be proved without a state or nationwide experiment in legalization. Americans are encouraged to accept it as an article of faith. There is, however, international evidence that argues for the opposite conclusion. In 1987, Zurich, Switzerland, opened Platzspitz Park as a haven for heroin addicts. The idea was based on tolerance. Initially, there were only a handful of addicts, but word quickly spread among Europe's growing heroin-addicted population that Platzspitz Park was a haven for drug users. The park quickly became a disaster area. Addicts poured in, but more important, local addiction soared. And the park itself became a dangerous place. Ultimately, reacting to public outrage, city officials reversed themselves and ended the experiment.

The Netherlands offers another example. Often hailed as the best model of social tolerance of drug use, the Netherlands has chosen largely not to enforce anti-drug laws and to tolerate drug use in specific areas, particularly certain sections of Amsterdam. The assumption was that tolerance and a good treatment program would deal with the addict population, which would gradually wither away when users understood the inherent dangers of drug use, and that drug use and again the crime associated with it would remain isolated. Instead, as in Platzspitz Park, addicts from all over Europe came to the Netherlands, and the local addict population has soared. Crime also has soared, both in the specified areas and more generally. Today, by some estimates, the Netherlands is the most crime-prone nation in Europe, and authorities are reconsidering many of their basic assumptions in the face of public pressure. Furthermore, Dutch efforts to license legal heroin use quickly ran aground amid huge increases in crime and overdose deaths, despite generous treatment and information programs. As one advocate of legalization admits, "We have a lot to learn from the Dutch."

CRIME AND SOCIAL PROBLEMS

Historical evidence in the United States also suggests that drug use would soar if drugs were legalized. Americans can examine the vast social experiment with drugs in the 1960s and 1970s. Liberal political leaders, the popular press, Hollywood, intellectuals, and other "opinion makers" downplayed the dangers of drug use, when they did not extol it, and pushed for nonenforcement of existing anti-drug laws. It was a pervasive social message: Drug use is a personal choice with no serious negative side effects or socially deleterious consequences. While not everyone went as far as Dr. Timothy Leary in celebrating the new age of a higher humanity thanks to LSD, the cumulative message was unmistakable. America's youth got the point. There was an explosion in use—despite widespread information on the negative health implications—followed by a crime wave, increased social violence, and growing health care costs. Drug traffickers also got the message, profiting handsomely.

Prohibition did not create this increase in crime and social problems. De facto legalization did. But according to legalization advocates, the reaction to the problem of drug addiction from the 1960s and 1970s was overblown by hysterical researchers, moralizing do-gooders, conservative politicians, and the mindless press; the health care costs of illegal drugs also allegedly were exaggerated. In short, the problem did not justify all the fuss. And based on the assumption that the present user population would not increase with legalization, they claim that future costs will not be as bad as projected, and will not be as bad as for tobacco or alcohol—or at least will be no worse if drugs are legalized.

Needless to say, these views are subject to challenge. There is nothing to justify a claim that the drug epidemic was the figment of narrow-minded moralizers, that it was not all that serious, and that the costs were exaggerated. The facts point to a very different conclusion. And there is nothing in the available evidence to show that society should not hold drug users to a measure of responsibility for their acts or continue to control access to dangerous drugs. . . .

THE TOBACCO AND ALCOHOL ANALOGY

Proponents of legalization argue that illegal drugs should be treated the same as tobacco and alcohol. This is another argument by analogy. Tobacco and alcohol are legal, and yet they are responsible for 500,000 premature deaths a year and staggering health care and allied costs. Therefore, because psychotropic drugs kill far fewer people at present levels of use—which supposedly will not increase—America should legalize them and treat the insignificant consequences that follow.

Proponents of this argument use a barrage of facts to show the sad consequences of legalized tobacco and alcohol, arguing that because tobacco and alcohol are legal and cause collateral damage, America should legalize psychoactive drugs. Not only is this illogical, it establishes no causal relationship between the elements. Indeed, the reverse can be argued: Prohibit the use of tobacco and alcohol because of the immense harm they do. Such a prohibition is not politically feasible in the case of tobacco, but it certainly is more logical than saying that because alcohol and tobacco take a terrible toll, a heavy toll from legalizing drugs is therefore acceptable.

One can imagine the storm of ridicule that would accompany a suggestion that business should be permitted to increase the production of environmentally unsafe wastes because firms already produce so much, or that enforcement of environmental laws should be made merely symbolic because so much damage has already been done. Such an argument could not be made seriously in public. Yet advocates of legalization seem to enjoy a certain cachet, especially among elite audiences, when they use the same brand of logic. If anything, the considerable social and economic costs of dealing with the legal use of tobacco and alcohol are substantive arguments for not adding to the collective woe by legalizing dangerous drugs. . . .

NOT AN INEVITABLE EVIL

Americans can never reasonably expect to eliminate drug production and use. Declaring war on murder will not end it, and there will be no end to the struggle against drug use. But neither is it possible to accept drug use as an inevitable evil. To do so would cause social chaos. Even most legalization advocates recognize the harm that drugs do and propose ways to lessen their effects. The difference is that they believe individual claims override community ones, that the evil of drug use is preferable to worse evil of oppressive and intrusive government, but their evidence is not compelling and their logic, even less so.

After seeing the results of widespread drug availability and use in the 1960s and 1970s, the American public demanded action. The action they demanded, and upon which they still insist, is to attack drug trafficking and punish use. They have not accepted the false notion that addiction is a victimless crime; too many families have been destroyed for that fiction to carry much weight. They still believe in individual obligations to balance individual rights. They are not prepared to honor claims on the public treasury to substitute therapy for responsibility.

Policy makers have an obligation to respect those opinions and to take them into account. To go against such widely and deeply held convictions may be the mark of statesmanship in some circumstances. The public can be wrong; and when clear-sighted analysis based on convincing evidence is available, genuine leaders act upon it no matter how overwhelming the public sentiment. In this case, however, statesmanship is not required; good sense is.

The public is right.

"There is . . . little reason . . . to suggest that legalizing the illegal drugs would produce a huge increase in the numbers of users of pleasure drugs or, more important, the numbers of abusers of such drugs."

LEGALIZING DRUGS WOULD NOT INCREASE DRUG ABUSE

Steven B. Duke and Albert C. Gross

Steven B. Duke and Albert C. Gross argue that the legalization of drugs would not lead to soaring increases in drug abuse. They do concede that, with lower prices for drugs, the use of marijuana and cocaine would increase moderately. However, they maintain that the use of other harmful drugs—especially alcohol—would decrease, leading to a net benefit for society. Duke is a law professor at Yale University in New Haven, Connecticut. Gross is a lawyer in San Diego, California.

As you read, consider the following questions:

1. According to Duke and Gross, how will legalization lead to an increase in drug use and yet a decrease in drug abuse at the same time?
2. What would happen to the practice of drug testing under legalization, according to the authors?
3. Why do Duke and Gross suggest that restrictions on the use of drugs by children would be more effectively enforced under legalization?

S ince eliminating (or greatly shrinking) the black market in drugs is the main object of legalization, drug prices under a system of legalization, even though taxed, must be kept much lower than they are now. When most commodities become cheaper, more people use them and those who used them before use more of them. That is true to some extent when the commodity is a pleasure drug. We observed that with the invention of crack in the mid-1980s, when the cost of a cocaine high was drastically reduced, bringing in hordes of new users. In July 1992, the New York Times reported that due in part to the recent abundance of heroin and cocaine (despite decades of drug war aimed at preventing it), drug dealers had cut the price of a $10 or "dime" bag of heroin to $5 and, in some parts of the city, reduced the price of a dose of crack to an all-time low of 75 cents. New York authorities believe that the reduced prices also accompanied increases in the numbers of both new users and abusers of cocaine. Heroin use also increased as prices declined, because users could afford to snort heroin rather than inject it and thus avoided the risk of AIDS and several other diseases related to intravenous drug use. Several studies show that the price of cigarettes—our most addictive drug—has a measurable impact upon consumption, especially long term: the higher the price, other things being equal, the less tobacco is smoked. Reducing the amount of money it takes to buy a dose of a drug is not the only cost reduction to the user contemplated by legalization. The user under legalization will no longer be a felon for using drugs and will no longer feel pressured to commit crimes in order to pay for the drugs used. Thus, in a broad sense, the "price" of drug use under legalization will be vastly reduced. There is undoubtedly a causal relationship between drug usage and drug prices, especially over the short term.

Legalizing the use of a drug that was previously criminal is also likely to have some influence in the direction of increasing consumption beyond its effects on the availability of drugs. Laws still have some impact upon the behavior of some citizens, even if such laws are widely disregarded by large segments of society. While legalizing drugs is not a statement that using drugs is desirable—the government regularly propagandizes against many activities that are legal, including smoking, dropping out of school, unsafe sex and so forth—legalization can be interpreted by some potential drug users as withdrawing condemnation, even as morally equating the use of newly legalized drugs with those already legal, such as tobacco and alcohol. This too can have a contributing influence on the consumption of previously illegal drugs. . . .

There is, therefore, a substantial likelihood that, *all other things remaining equal*, legalization will be accompanied by an increase in the consumption of newly legalized drugs. But there is also little reason, and no support in what followed the repeal of alcohol prohibition, to suggest that legalizing the illegal drugs would produce a huge increase in the numbers of users of pleasure drugs or, more important, the numbers of *abusers* of such drugs. One who neither smokes tobacco nor drinks alcohol is extremely unlikely to become a user of any of the other pleasure drugs (caffeine aside). While there are surely some teetotalers or occasional light drinkers who would become addicted to heroin or cocaine under a system of legalization, their numbers are almost certainly small. The major reasons why people desist from smoking and drinking—health, social stigma, morality, aesthetics—are also applicable to other pleasure drugs.

REDUCTION OF ALCOHOL ABUSE

The potential new users of legalized drugs are therefore people who are now deterred by the price of these drugs or by the criminality of their use, but who nonetheless drink or smoke cigarettes. To the extent that such persons were to substitute newly legalized pleasure drugs for tobacco or alcohol, they would be better off from a bodily health standpoint, and so would those who come into contact with them. Cocaine or heroin users do not pollute the air and rarely beat up their spouses or children while intoxicated on those drugs.

Most of the people who would abuse cocaine or heroin if it were legalized, but who do not now abuse these drugs, are already abusing alcohol, killing themselves and others by the tens of thousands every year. They would be less likely to kill themselves with drugs if they used less alcohol, even if they used more cocaine or heroin, and would be much less likely to kill the rest of us.

It seems clear that increased consumption of marijuana or heroin, all other conditions remaining the same, will result in a reduction in the consumption of alcohol. The psychoactive effects of such drugs are sufficiently similar to alcohol, among a large number of users, that they are to a substantial extent substitutes. What is less clear is whether such a relationship exists between cocaine and alcohol. A great many cocaine users also consume alcohol while taking cocaine; the two drugs are apparently complementary, one being a depressant and the other a stimulant. Alcohol, which is cheap, may augment the effects of cocaine, which is expensive. Alcohol thus seems to play a role similar to that of Hamburger Helper. It is not as good as the real thing, but it helps to stretch out the real thing with tolerable diluting effects. We think it is likely, however, that increased use of cocaine will not be accompanied by an increased use of alcohol but rather a reduction. If cocaine is inexpensive, as it would be under legalization, there would be little incentive to use alcohol as a stretcher or helper of cocaine. More important, perhaps, combining either heroin and cocaine with alcohol is dangerous. Most deaths from "overdoses" of cocaine and heroin may in reality be overdoses of alcohol (or barbiturates) and cocaine or heroin (or both). Users would be better informed about the risks of drug synergy under legalization. The kick or sensation that alcohol adds to cocaine would not be worth the risks in a legalized system, since cocaine itself would be approximately the same price per intoxicating dose as alcohol.

CHOOSING TO QUIT

The very substantial reductions in numbers of alcohol and tobacco users over the past few decades demonstrates that people are capable of avoiding drugs that they know are bad for them, even if the government says they are legal and they are widely advertised as the key to success and happiness. As federal judge Robert W. Sweet observed in a 1989 speech urging drug legalization, "If our society can learn to stop using butter, it should be able to cut down on cocaine."

Whether Americans choose to avoid recreational drugs in the first place or to quit using or abusing them is linked to the quality of their lives and their perceived prospects for a rewarding life without drug use or abuse. This is clearly demonstrated by recent data about illegal-drug use. Illegal-drug use has been reduced drastically in the past few years among white middle and upper classes—but hardly or not at all among ethnic minorities, who largely inhabit our inner cities. Many of those users see nothing but a bleak future before them. They have little to lose by drug abuse, and they proceed to lose it.

In sum, the drug market is already saturated with a combination of legal and illegal drugs. Virtually everyone who now wants to get high already does so. Legalization may significantly alter market shares among the now legal and illegal drugs, but it is unlikely to create a strong surge in new demand for psychoactive drugs. As Michael S. Gazzaniga, professor of neuroscience at Dartmouth Medical School, puts it, "There is a base rate of drug abuse, and it is [presently] achieved one way or another."

Even if heroin, cocaine and marijuana legalization increased substantially the number of users of such drugs and even their total drug consumption, the number of abusers of such drugs could still be diminished by legalization. The drugs used would probably be less potent than those now available and therefore less addictive and less damaging. Users of legal drugs also have many advantages over users of illegal drugs that help them to resist frequent, heavy use. They need not be criminals or outcasts to use the drugs. They are less likely to acquire serious or incapacitating illnesses from drug use. They need not steal to buy their drugs; they can work at a regular, legitimate job. Legal-drug use, therefore, is far more compatible with the personal ties, extrinsic resources and general well-being that support efforts to resist drug abuse.

OTHER POSSIBLE RISKS

There are no other major risks of legalization apart from increased consumption of drugs. All other risks are subsidiaries. Some of the derivative risks deserve mention, however. If legalization were to produce major long-run increases in the numbers of psychoactive-drug abusers—an assumption we have difficulty making for reasons already set forth—a number of concrete adverse consequences might follow. Many heroin and cocaine abusers, like alcoholics, have difficulty holding jobs or handling other significant responsibilities. Some of them—like many alcoholics—seem all but immune to treatment or other therapeutic interventions. Such persons have more than their share of health problems, and could put an additional strain on our health care systems. If legalization were to produce hundreds of thousands of new addicts who were incapable of functioning in the society, along with the mentally ill, alcohol and other drug-abusing derelicts who already inhabit our cities, this would indeed be a major cost of legalization. But for reasons already discussed, neither common sense nor experience supports the likelihood of such a scenario. . . .

DRUG TESTING WOULD BE MORE ACCEPTABLE

Another subsidiary risk is that, if use of newly legalized drugs became far more widespread than at present, there would be greatly enlarged safety risks to nonusers. Automobiles, trucks, airplanes, factory machinery would be operated by people whose capacities were significantly impaired by drugs. But as we have noted, the major impairments are produced by alcohol, not the other drugs. If legalization diverts users from alcohol, we may even have safer highways and airways as a result. But it is, in any event, possible to prohibit driving and piloting by drug-impaired persons in a state of legalization. In fact, it would be less difficult under legalization because impaired operators would have less reason than they now do—when mere use of the drugs is a serious crime—to hide their condition. Drug testing is now commonplace—far more so than we would like—but in a state of legalization, drug testing by employers and traffic police would be much less objectionable, since it would not expose the person tested to a charge of a serious felony. Moreover, modern technology is capable of producing portable devices to test cognitive, perceptual and motor capacities. Such tests are far more relevant to one's ability to operate machinery than a test to determine the presence, or even the quantity, of drugs in one's blood, breath or urine.

The Ability to Quit

It is arguable that decriminalizing drugs while restricting access, employing warnings, and increasing awareness of their potential hazards would lead to a reduction in usage.

Most people who use cocaine and marijuana are occasional users. Most users have no trouble stopping if they decide to. Only three percent of the people who have tried cocaine reported problems giving it up. With marijuana, the number of people who use the drug is much higher, but the proportion of those who report difficulty in giving up the drug, even after a long period of heavy usage, is negligible. The most highly addictive of these illegal drugs are the opiates and their derivatives (particularly heroin). We do not have good data on the addiction rate among opium users, but we do know that when opium was legally and easily available to addicts through medical doctors, as it was in Great Britain until the 1970s, the illegal drug market and the number of new addicts were minuscule compared with the United States.

A comparison of the addictive qualities of illegal drugs with tobacco and alcohol is informative. A survey of high school seniors asked those who admitted to using marijuana, cocaine, and cigarettes if they had ever had difficulty stopping. Less than four percent reported difficulty stopping cocaine, while seven percent reported difficulty with marijuana and 18% with quitting cigarette smoking. . . .

If the drugs were legal and the stigma of criminality were not attached to the user, problem drug users would seek the help they need.

William J. Chambliss, *Social Justice*, Summer 1995.

Legalizing drugs does not require that impaired driving also be made legal. Drivers who are seriously impaired, for whatever reasons, should not drive and should be punished if they do so.

It is sometimes said that legalization will produce more "crack babies" or other infants whose health is seriously damaged by their mothers' drug use during pregnancy. But much—perhaps most—of the damage done to such babies comes from their mothers' neglect of nutrition and hygiene, combined with the fact that many of them have no prenatal medical care. Fear of criminal prosecution keeps many such mothers away from prenatal care when it is available. Moreover, most drug-treatment programs, believe it or not, refuse access to pregnant mothers! Such idiocy would stop under any rational system of legalization.

INCREASED EXPERIMENTATION BY TEENAGERS

Finally, what about our children? Is it possible that the high cost of illegal drugs is a significant deterrent to drug experimentation by America's teenagers? If this cost were drastically reduced, a substantial segment of such deterrables might experiment with newly legalized drugs and become hooked. What we have already said about adults applies here as well. Children who do not drink or smoke will not use cocaine or heroin, however cheap it is. Many of those who do drink or smoke, and are interested in expanding their use of drugs, already have tried marijuana and many have tried cocaine. The price of experimental quantities of illegal drugs is already well within the reach of most teenagers.

Moreover, as difficult as it may be for some to contemplate, even if legalization produced a substantial increase in juvenile experimentation with marijuana, heroin or cocaine, the juveniles themselves, and the rest of society, might still be better off. Tobacco and alcohol are especially harmful to children's bodies; a reduction in the use of those drugs by juveniles would be a great advance, even if achieved by some increase in the use of other drugs.

We would continue to criminalize the distribution of drugs, including tobacco and alcohol, to children. But since drug use among adults would be lawful, we could concentrate our law-enforcement resources on purveyors of drugs to children, and we could be far more successful in that endeavor, having narrowed our focus, than we are today. It is not true that anything a society permits adults to do cannot effectively be denied children, and that, as a result, adults who encourage children to engage in such "adult" activities cannot be condemned. Sex between adults and children is severely condemned in America, while sex between unmarried adults is not even a misdemeanor in most states. We would treat the distribution of drugs to children like statutory rape, and put people in prison for it. Under today's prohibition that rarely happens.

THE BALANCE OF BENEFITS AND COSTS

We think almost any one of the . . . benefits we have sketched above outweighs the risks of legalization—which are not great. When all benefits are combined, the case for legalization becomes overwhelming. If legalization is too large a leap, courageous governors and a courageous president could give us many of the benefits of legalization simply by de-escalating the war. Cut the drug-law-enforcement budgets by two thirds . . . , stop civil forfeitures, grant executive clemency to most of the nonviolent drug violators stuffing our prisons, and much of the evil of prohibition will disappear. When the benefits of de-escalation are experienced, the nation will then be ready for de jure reform.

The meekest among us must admit that the case for legalizing marijuana is overwhelming. Jimmy Carter was right when he proposed decriminalization during his presidency. We would all be better off if he had succeeded. Marijuana poses some health risks, but far less than tobacco or alcohol, and it substitutes for and therefore competes with both alcohol and tobacco. Pending the legalization of marijuana, our nation's chief executives and law-enforcement officers should put a stop to all prosecution for marijuana possession or trafficking, and open the prison doors for all who are there solely for such offenses. Even an ardent prohibitionist ought to agree with this proposal. Everyone agrees that cocaine and heroin are worse drugs, by any standards, than marijuana. If marijuana is legalized, the drug warriors could then focus their resources on the war against "hard" drugs.

The case for legalization is strong; the case for de-escalating the drug war is overwhelming.

"Legalization will likely lead to increases in drug use, addiction and drug-related death."

LEGALIZING DRUGS WOULD INCREASE DRUG ABUSE

Robert L. DuPont

Robert L. DuPont is a former director of the National Institute on Drug Abuse and a former "drug czar," or director of the Office of National Drug Control Policy. In the following viewpoint, DuPont argues that the inevitable result of the legalization of drugs would be increased drug use, along with increased addiction and death rates. Neither the preprohibition experience with drugs in the United States nor the current experiments with legalization in other countries provide any evidence that legalization would be beneficial, according to DuPont. DuPont is currently a clinical professor of psychiatry at Georgetown University School of Medicine in Washington, D.C.

As you read, consider the following questions:

1. According to DuPont, which has greater costs to society, drugs that are legal or drugs that are illegal?
2. What does DuPont conclude about the Dutch experiment with the legalization of marijuana?
3. In DuPont's view, why are most drug treatment professionals against legalization?

From Robert L. DuPont, "Will Legalizing Drugs Benefit Public Health? No," Priorities, vol. 7, no. 2, 1995. Reprinted with permission from Priorities, a publication of the American Council on Science and Health, 1995 Broadway, 2nd Floor, New York, NY 10023-5860.

Proposals for drug legalization are rooted in the belief that drug prohibition does not work. Legalization advocates point out that the prohibition of alcohol failed in the United States two generations ago. They argue that the use of illicit drugs is widespread despite prohibition and that the high costs and negative consequences of that prohibition—ranging from costs for police and prisons to the loss of privacy caused by drug testing in many settings, notably the workplace—are unreasonably high prices to pay for an ineffective policy. But while prohibition has not been the perfect solution to the drug problem, legalization will likely lead to increases in drug use, addiction and drug-related death.

The range of available options within both general categories, drug legalization and drug prohibition, is wide. It is useful to look at the big picture to examine (and question) the whole spectrum of options. In general, we can ask: Is prohibition working? Is it cost effective? Does legalization offer a reasonable alternative to prohibition?

There are three models for legalization that can help us sketch an answer to these fundamental questions. The first is a look back at life in the United States a hundred years ago, when addicting drugs were sold like toothpaste and candy. The second is derived from observing the recent trends in the rates of the use of both legal and illegal drugs in the United States and comparing the costs generated by the drugs that now are legal for adults—tobacco and alcohol—and those that are not—marijuana, cocaine, heroin and others. The third is a look at the experiences of other countries that have experimented with legalization. Examining these models gives us valuable perspective as we consider the possibility of lifting prohibition and replacing it with one of the many options for drug legalization.

A LOOK AT THE AMERICAN EXPERIENCE

The American experience with drugs at the end of the 19th century demonstrated the serious problems that can be caused by the general use of a wide range of legally available drugs. These problems were, finally, judged unacceptable by Americans of that day. Prohibition was the result of a nonpartisan public outcry over the negative effects of unrestricted drug use. Thus, the prohibition of heroin and cocaine did not cause widespread drug use; widespread drug use caused prohibition.

Furthermore, the prohibition of drugs has been almost universally supported politically in the United States and throughout the world for more than half a century. The single exception was, of course, the prohibition of alcohol.

The goal of a drug policy is to reduce harm. Alcohol and to-bacco cause far more harm in the U.S. than all illegal drugs combined. Deaths in the United States from alcohol are estimated at about 125,000 per year. Tobacco use causes about 420,000 deaths a year. Deaths resulting from all illicit drugs combined are fewer than 10,000 per year.

TABLE 1: ECONOMIC COSTS OF ADDICTION IN THE UNITED STATES, 1990

	Illicit Drugs	Alcohol	Tobacco
Total Cost (billions)	$66.9	$98.6	$72.0
Medical Care (%)	3.2 (4.8)	10.5 (10.7)	20.2 (28.0)
Lost Productivity (%)	8.0 (11.9)	36.6 (37.1)	6.8 (9.0)
Death (%)	3.4 (5.1)	33.6 (34.1)	45.0 (63.0)
Crime (%)	46.0 (68.8)	15.8 (16.0)	0.0 (0.0)
AIDS (%)	6.3 (9.4)	2.1 (2.1)	0.0 (0.0)

TABLE 2: AMERICAN DRUG USE IN THE PRIOR 30 DAYS (IN MILLIONS)

	1985	1993	Decline from 1985 to 1993
Drugs Legal for Adults			
Alcohol	113	103	9%
Cigarettes	60	50	17%
The Most Widely Used Drugs That Are Illegal for All			
Marijuana	18	9	50%
Cocaine	6	1.3	78%

Source: Robert L. DuPont, Priorities, vol. 7, no. 2, 1995.

Similarly, the costs to society of alcohol use in the United States in 1990 were estimated at $98.6 billion a year; the costs of tobacco smoking were estimated to be $72 billion; and the 1990 estimated costs of all illicit drugs—including the costs of prohibition—were $66.9 billion.

To put these statistics another way: Whether the standard is drug-caused deaths or drug-related economic costs, the drugs that are legal for adults (alcohol and tobacco) cause far more harm than do all currently illegal drugs combined (see Table 1).

Table 2 shows figures for 1985 and 1993 of the number of

people in the United States who said they had used legal and/or illegal drugs in the previous 30 days. The table also shows the decline in the rates of use of all these substances in the years from 1985 to 1993. The prohibited drugs were used at lower levels and showed greater reductions in use over that time span than either cigarettes or alcohol.

Note, in Table 1, that the economic cost of illicit drugs is primarily related to crime: Almost 70 percent of the $66.9 billion total cost of illicit drugs in 1990 was the cost of prohibition. At the same time, crime produced only 16 percent of the cost to society of alcohol and zero percent of the cost generated by tobacco use.

The costs of medical care, lost productivity and death stand in dramatic contrast to the crime costs, however. Those costs taken together totaled $14.6 billion for all illegal drugs, $80.7 billion for alcohol and $72 billion for tobacco. These figures show clearly that when drugs are legalized, they are used more widely—and the total costs of their use go up when compared to the costs of drugs still under prohibition. The costs of legal drugs are primarily costs related to medical care, lost productivity and death. . . .

COSTS PER USER

Some advocates of the legalization of now-illegal drugs claim that those drugs do not produce health costs on the scale of those produced by alcohol and tobacco, but the data show that illicit drugs produce higher levels of health and productivity costs *per user* than do legal drugs.

The United States has about 103 million current users of alcohol, 50 million current users of tobacco and 12 million current users of illicit drugs. The health-related costs per user per year, exclusive of crime costs, are $798 for users of alcohol, $1,440 for users of tobacco—and $1,742 for users of illicit drugs.

Under prohibition, the costs to society of illegal drugs are lower, overall, than the costs of legal drugs; and the costs of illicit drugs show up primarily in police and corrections budgets. Prohibition is currently reducing the total costs generated by drugs such as marijuana, cocaine and heroin. But human suffering—and health-care costs—would rise dramatically if those drugs were as readily and legally available as alcohol and tobacco are now.

Those who support legalization widely praise the Dutch for permitting the purchase of marijuana for use by those over age 15. But the Dutch saw a 250 percent increase in adolescent marijuana use between 1984 and 1992. During the same period, American youth reduced their marijuana use by two thirds. Furthermore, between 1991 and 1993 the Dutch saw a 30 percent increase in registered marijuana addicts.

The evidence from the Netherlands suggests that if the United States were to legalize currently illicit drugs, the number of users would likely increase from the present 12 million to something like the 50 million who use tobacco or even the 103 million who use alcohol. The current prohibition in the United States works reasonably well in reducing both the amount and the costs of addictive drug use. Legalization would result both in the increased use of no-longer-illegal drugs and in more harm, which would be expressed in greater social costs.

WIDER USE EQUALS WIDER HARM

Those who would reform drug laws who also support harm-reduction objectives should focus their efforts on alcohol and tobacco—the two drugs responsible for the major part of the drug-caused harm now taking place in the United States and throughout the world. Those two substances are not causing the most harm because they are more dangerous—or more attractive—than marijuana, cocaine or heroin. Alcohol and tobacco are, in fact, less attractive to many experienced drug users; and they are much less dangerous than marijuana, cocaine and heroin. Alcohol and tobacco produce more harm than all of the illegal drugs combined—even when you include the costs of prohibition—simply because alcohol and tobacco are so much more widely used. Furthermore, alcohol and tobacco are more widely used by children because their use is legal for adults.

If all drugs were declared completely legal, many people would still choose not to use them, just as many adults choose not to use alcohol and tobacco today. And even under the most severe prohibition, some people still choose to use prohibited drugs. The question, however, is this: Would legalization, when compared to prohibition, increase both the number of drug users and the social harm produced by the use of these substances? The answer is yes.

THE COSTS OF PROHIBITION

Those who support legalization correctly point out that prohibition is an expensive strategy. Making the consumption of marijuana, cocaine, heroin and other drugs illegal costs society large sums of money for everything from police and prisons to the incentives that prohibition-inflated drug prices provide to illicit drug traffickers. There are costs, too, in the loss of privacy: Drug tests are widely used in the criminal-justice system, the workplace and elsewhere.

Those who support prohibition do not help their case by denying the magnitude of these costs. The question to ask is this: Are the high costs of prohibition justified in terms of reduced harm and an improved quality of life for most citizens? The evidence is clear; the answer is yes. Prohibition is worth its high costs.

THE VIEWS OF DRUG-TREATMENT PROFESSIONALS

One curious aspect of the legalization controversy is that people who are involved in drug treatment almost all oppose legalization. One would think that if they were operating in their own self interest, these people would welcome legalization; after all, it would substantially increase the need for the treatment of addiction. However, drug-treatment professionals generally oppose drug legalization because their dedication to the welfare of drug users is more powerful than their dedication to their own narrow economic interests.

Talk, too, to drug abusers in treatment or to those who have successfully developed solid, personal recovery programs. Few of them support legalization; they know that such an approach would make life harder for them and for all other recovering former users.

LIFE AFTER LEGALIZATION: A PROJECTION

Since many thoughtful people have proposed the legalization of drugs as a solution to the war we are waging against the financial, social, medical and political ravages of drug abuse, I would like to share my own projection of the results of such a decision. Here is my fantasy of life after drug legalization:

Let's say some community or nation were to give it a try, putting heroin, cocaine, LSD and the whole modern menu of addicting drugs on sale in local markets. The results of the experiment would not be long in coming, and they wouldn't be hard to predict.

First the good news: As a result of drug legalization, crime costs for prisons, courts and police would fall. Tax revenues would rise, and the illegal market for the newly legal drugs would be reduced.

Then the bad news: Health and productivity costs would increase dramatically, and the net costs to society would rise substantially. Worse, the human costs from drug use would rise over time as more people who tried the drugs used them and became addicted. And the highest costs of legalization would be paid by those most vulnerable to addiction: the young and the disadvantaged.

If any community in the world would be so foolish as to try the outright legalization of marijuana, cocaine, heroin and LSD, we might have less discussion of this thoroughly unworkable and dangerous—but endlessly seductive—idea.

But this fantasy of drug legalization is not merely speculative. The scenario has already been played out in the real world. In 1987 the Swiss opened a drug bazaar, called "Needle Park," for a few hundred addicts. By 1992, 20,000 addicts had swarmed to Switzerland, and that nation's heroin death rate had become Europe's highest. That same year, in the face of public outrage, the Swiss police closed Needle Park.

THE BETTER WAY

It has often been said that democracy—although a messy, expensive and flawed system of government—is better than any of the alternatives. The prohibition of currently illegal drugs is also a messy, expensive and flawed system; but, like democracy, it is better than the alternatives. This is not to say that drug-prohibition strategies cannot be improved; they almost certainly can be. But abundant evidence gathered from many societies over many years has shown that, in general, the prohibition of drugs such as marijuana, cocaine and heroin is a reasonable and generally effective way to deal with a difficult human problem.

"Most of the crime associated with drugs derives from their illegality. Making all drugs legal would, of course, define most of these offenses out of existence."

LEGALIZING DRUGS WOULD LEAD TO A REDUCTION IN CRIME

Theodore Vallance

In the following viewpoint, Theodore Vallance argues that some form of regulated legalization must replace the current war on drugs. He claims that the war on drugs is responsible not only for crime committed by addicts, drug traffickers, and dealers, but also for corruption and bribery in the justice system. Legalization would completely eliminate the motivation for all drug-related crimes, Vallance maintains. Vallance is a professor emeritus at Pennsylvania State University and the author of *Prohibition's Second Failure: The Quest for a Rational and Humane Drug Policy.*

As you read, consider the following questions:

1. Why do addicts commit large numbers of crimes, according to Vallance?
2. In the author's view, what tempts some police into drug-related corruption?
3. What does Vallance recommend as the first phase or trial of legalization?

From Theodore Vallance, "A Most Complex Problem." This article appeared in the January 1995 issue and is reprinted with permission from the *World & I*, a publication of The Washington Times Corporation; copyright ©1995.

L iterally millions of lawbreakings occur daily. Most are committed by the estimated 20 million users of illegal drugs
who generate more than a million arrests annually. More newsworthy are crimes to obtain money for buying drugs. The average heroin addict needs $10,000 a year to sustain the habit, and
nearly all heroin addicts commit predatory crimes: muggings,
burglaries, and occasional associated killings. In Miami, 356
heroin users admitted committing nearly 120,000 criminal acts
in a single year—an average of 332 crimes per person, which
looks much like full-time employment. Studies of heroin users
in other cities produce similar results.

Users of cocaine and other nonnarcotic drugs contribute
their share of predatory crimes, plus bank and credit card fraud
and forgery. Interviews of 500 cocaine hot-line callers showed
45 percent of them reporting that they had stolen to support
their cocaine habits. The data on predatory crime are nearly endless. The subsidy for drug prices that prohibition provides too
often requires that money be gotten from activities beyond
one's regular employment, especially if that employment is er-
ratic or poorly paid. Still more dramatic are the shoot-outs between drug merchants as they try to sustain or expand market
share. Because disagreements about drug-selling turf can't be
appealed to the courts of law like violations of other business
agreements, resort to the court of the gun is common. . . .

YIELDING TO TEMPTATION

If you were offered an opportunity to make in one month your
expected total lifetime earnings just by doing a few unlikely-to-
be-discovered but illegal acts, would you be tempted? Of course
not! But many people would—and do pick up the opportunity.
When the business at hand is illegal and thus puts its practition-
ers at risk of arrest and imprisonment, one obvious defense is to
persuade those who would enforce the law to be less than thorough in their duties. Some policemen in every large American
city earn extra income from drug dealers by tipping them off to
impending raids or reporting the presence of outside competi-
tors in their turf. A New York study estimated that 40 percent of
the price of cocaine in one neighborhood represented the cost of
paying cops to direct their vision away from drug transactions.

Cash seized in drug raids offers heavy temptation to the arresting officers; eighteen Los Angeles County sheriff's deputies
were suspended in 1989 for yielding to temptation. More recently, several New York policemen were charged with operating
their own business of distributing cocaine seized in raids. Temp-

tations for this kind of behavior are strengthened by the demoralizing conviction that the street-level drug war accomplishes little, that a heavy crackdown in one neighborhood simply moves the drug trade, alive and well, to another. And it's not just police who are corrupted. An assistant U.S. attorney in New York State stole drugs and money from government supplies and was duly convicted, and a federal judge was convicted recently of bribery in a drug case.

MORAL CONFLICTS

Regrettably, we have come to accept bribery and other corruptions as a normal part of politics and law enforcement, undermining public faith in the criminal justice system (Why should I obey the law when thousands are getting away with murder? Should I bother to report the bribe that I know about when I know there won't be any prosecution?) and encouraging the rise of vigilantism. Another moral conflict with which we continue to live is the hypocrisy in our current policy: Alcohol, nicotine, and caffeine are okay, kind of like apple pie. But those other drugs are morally bad, as are the people who use them—and not just because it is wrong to break laws. Somehow, they differ morally from the rest of us (booze drinking) law-abiders. . . .

HARM REDUCTION

Somewhere between the extremes of instant free-market unregulated legalization of all currently illegal drugs and redoubling law-enforcement efforts over and over again must lie a policy that would enlarge some of the good features in our present practices and reduce many of the bad ones. The aim of such a policy can be termed "harm reduction," recognizing that drugs will always be with us, like them or not. Such a policy would have to placate moralists who insist that "drugs in themselves are bad," as well as libertarians who argue for the individual's right to do to himself what he will. It should appear reasonable to politicians facing voters convinced that there is nothing good about drug-law reform and unconcerned about what costs must be borne to stamp out illegal drugs. In a peaceful and rational world, we should like to have a drug policy that minimizes harms of many kinds: economic, social, and moral. It should be politically tenable, and its rules should be acceptable to most people. But let's go from this comforting abstraction to prospects in the real world.

So large and complex an industry as illegal drugs and other, dependent industries will not readily relinquish economic, political, or moral turf. Thousands of people make legitimate livings from illegal drugs: The Drug Enforcement Administration (DEA) alone employs more than 5,000 people, and the individual states have their own DEAs. Many more thousands are to varying degrees prohibition-dependent: prosecuting and defense attorneys, prison builders, guards and administrators, employees and owners of the billion-dollar drug-testing business. One could even list tobacco and alcohol merchants, whose business might suffer competition from quality producers of less-dangerous recreational drugs. (Take note that after the Twenty-first Amendment turned over control of alcohol to the states, bootleggers worked hard in several states to keep alcohol illegal.)

DRUG PROHIBITION AND CRIME

Drug prohibition, like liquor prohibition, makes it profitable for criminal organizations to supply them and leaves addicts with no source of supply but criminals.

It is the prohibition which generates the crime, not only the crimes committed as rival gangs compete for market turf, but also the corruption of law enforcement, prosecutors and judges.

Charley Reese, *Conservative Chronicle*, August 6, 1997.

It cannot be refuted that most of the crime associated with drugs derives from their illegality. Making all drugs legal would, of course, define most of these offenses out of existence. But more significant is the fact that drug-related crime would lose its motivational base: the violent crime associated with defending turf and getting money to support habits, plus the corruption of police, courts, and other public officials.

LEGALIZATION MUST COME

The many proposals for alleviating the drug problem are far too complex for detailed review here, but a commentary on some major ideas is offered. My own review of the facts and principles convinces me that some form of regulated legalization must come, preceded and accompanied by extensive education about the risks of extensive drug use—reflecting the success of recent efforts in educating people to the hazards of smoking tobacco and drinking alcohol. But before adopting a new policy, here are some of the contingent questions whose answers must be broadly understood. How would legalization affect drug use? Which drugs should be legalized and on what time schedule? How should the drug market be regulated? Can juvenile access and subsequent addiction be prevented? Would drug use be permitted everywhere, or should some restrictions be adopted? How can advertising be controlled? What procedures for regulating drug use in the workplace should be adopted? . . .

Not a Drug-Free Society

Drug use might go up, though experience in the Netherlands and in the ten American states that decriminalized the personal use of marijuana in the 1970s suggests otherwise. Treatment for abuse would be more readily sought were abusers not at risk of arrest. Drug use would not disappear; attaining a drug-free society is as feasible as attaining a sex-free society; drug use and sex are aspects of human life to be appreciated and enjoyed with restraint, not stamped out.

Early regulated legalization of marijuana, including especially its use for medicinal purposes, would test legalization's feasibility and anticipate possible problems in legalizing other drugs.

Juvenile Access

On market regulation, unfettered distribution could attract children unaware of the risks of drug use. Having the federal government as sole distributor would avoid First Amendment issues about advertising and preclude inconsistencies among state-operated systems.

Restricting juvenile access would be as difficult as it is now for nicotine and alcohol, but serious enforcement of existing laws and practices could become effective. Banning vending machines selling tobacco and other drugs (can you imagine the flap such a proposal would raise?) could defeat today's easy access by juveniles to tobacco as well. Licensing of both sellers and buyers could help enforce age rules and limit volume of sales.

Restricting advertising raises constitutional free-speech issues that the courts have yet to resolve. Truth-in-labeling rules, including wording akin to the surgeon general's warning on cigarette packages, could counteract some promotions, but the best defense will probably be a solid educational offense.

Employee Assistance

Problems of drug use in the workplace can easily be incorporated in established employee-assistance programs. Smart firms know that helping employees deal with problems like alcoholism, compulsive gambling, family strife, and personal financial management can produce major savings in the form of reduced absenteeism, reduced turnover, and generally happier employees. If drugs were legal and the user largely free from stigma and the risk of being arrested or fired, employees would be more willing to use the assistance programs already available to them.

The tough issues and the necessity for making distasteful trade-offs remain. I leave the reader to ponder: What do you think we should do about this problem?

| "Although crimes associated with obtaining drugs might decrease with legalization, other crimes, especially violent crimes, would increase."

LEGALIZING DRUGS WOULD NOT LEAD TO A REDUCTION IN CRIME

Gerald W. Lynch and Roberta Blotner

Many critics of the current war on drugs claim that the legalization of drugs may result in some increased drug use, but that it also would drastically reduce the crime rate. In the following viewpoint, Gerald W. Lynch and Roberta Blotner challenge this view, arguing that increased drug use would lead to an increase in violent crimes such as murder, child abuse, and suicide. Lynch is president of the John Jay College of Criminal Justice, a unit of the City University of New York. Blotner is director of CUNY's substance-abuse prevention programs.

As you read, consider the following questions:
1. How do Lynch and Blotner use alcohol and tobacco addiction rates to support their claim that drug addiction would increase under legalization?
2. Why did the Zurich experiment with decriminalizing drugs fail, according to the authors?
3. What prevention strategies do Lynch and Blotner favor?

Reprinted, with permission, from Gerald W. Lynch and Roberta Blotner, "Legalizing Drugs Is Not the Answer," *America*, February 13, 1993.

In "The Challenge of Legalizing Drugs," Joseph P. Kane, S.J., in the August 8, 1992 *America*, presents a compelling description of the devastation wreaked on our society by drug abuse, but draws some troubling conclusions supporting the legalization of drugs. Father Kane argues that illegal drugs promote the proliferation of crime because of the huge profits associated with their import and sales. Violence and murder have increased dramatically as dealers and gangs compete for turf and drug profits. Youngsters are attracted to selling drugs in order to earn more money than they could ever hope to earn in legitimate jobs. Addicts steal to pay for their drugs. The criminal justice system is overwhelmed by the increasing number of drug arrests.

He further argues that because drugs are illegal, addicts are treated as criminals rather than as sick people in need of help. Addicts are often arrested and processed through the criminal justice system rather than offered legitimate rehabilitation or treatment. Finally, he states that illegal drugs exploit the poor, whose struggle to survive makes drug dealing a sometimes necessary alternative.

The solution to the problem, he concludes, is to legalize drugs while at the same time 1) changing attitudes within our society about drugs, 2) changing laws and public policy, and 3) providing drug education and treatment to all those who want it. While Father Kane's description of the toll drugs are taking on our society and our citizens is poignant, the solution to this problem is not legalization.

An Increase in Use

Legalizing drugs will almost certainly increase their use. This has been well documented in a number of studies. J.F. Mosher points out that alcohol usage and rates of liver disease declined significantly during Prohibition. Moreover, following repeal of the 18th Amendment, the number of drinkers in the United States increased by 60 percent.

The most widely abused drugs in our society are tobacco, alcohol and prescription drugs—the legal drugs and those which are most widely available. A recent report issued by the Federal Government states that approximately 57 million people in this country are addicted to cigarettes, 18 million are addicted to alcohol and 10 million are abusing psychotherapeutic drugs. By comparison, crack, heroin and hallucinogens each account for one million addicts. Further, the report states that every day in this country 1,000 people die of smoking-related illnesses, 550 die of alcohol-related accidents and diseases, while 20 die of drug overdoses and drug-related homicides. In addition, the annual costs of health care and lost productivity to employers are estimated at $600 billion for alcoholism and $60 billion for tobacco-related ailments. For all illegal drugs, however, the comparable cost is an estimated $40 billion. These data clearly demonstrate that the drugs which are most available are the most abused, the most dangerous and the most costly.

As the number of people using drugs increases, babies born to addicted mothers will increase as well. According to a report issued by the New York City Public Schools in 1991, during the preceding 10 years babies born to substance-abusing mothers increased 3,000 percent. It is estimated that each year approximately 10,000 babies are born exposed to drugs. With greater availability of drugs, it is inevitable that more babies will be born to substance-abusing mothers. According to guidelines offered by the Children Prenatally Exposed to Drugs Program of the Los Angeles Unified School District, the following are among the characteristics of the child prenatally exposed to drugs: neurological problems, affective disorders, poor concentration, delayed language development, impaired social skills, difficulty in play. The extent to which children of addicted fathers may be impaired is not yet known. Legalizing drugs will surely compound the tragedy to our society of these most innocent victims.

AN INCREASE IN CRIME

Drug legalization would not eliminate crime. Although crimes associated with obtaining drugs might decrease with legalization, other crimes, especially violent crimes, would increase. As many as 80 percent of violent crimes involve alcohol and drugs. A number of studies have demonstrated the relationship between drugs and homicides, automobile deaths, child abuse and sexual abuse. It is estimated that drugs and alcohol are involved in 50 percent to 75 percent of cases of suicidal behavior. According to recent pharmacological research, certain drugs, especially cocaine, have the tendency to elicit violent behavior because of changes that take place in the neurotransmitter systems of the brain.

Many experts think that unless there were free access to unlimited quantities of drugs, there would be a black market even after legalization. Drugs, even if legal, would still cost money. Since many addicts cannot maintain jobs, they would continue to engage in stealing and prostitution to pay for drugs and would continue to subject their families and friends to abuse.

Experiments with the decriminalization of drugs have failed.

A case in point is Zurich, Switzerland. There the city set aside a park, the Platzspitz, in which drugs were decriminalized and were available with no legal consequences. Health care was made accessible and clean syringes were supplied. It was hoped that there would be a reduction in crime, better health care for addicts and containment of the problem to a defined area of the city. The experiment failed dramatically.

As reported in the *New York Times* on February 11, 1992, and London's *Financial Times* on January 4, 1992, Zurich's drug-related crime and violence actually increased. Drug users and dealers converged on the Swiss city from other countries throughout Europe. The health-care system was overwhelmed as drug users had to be resuscitated. As drug dealers began to compete for business, the cost of drugs decreased. One addict was quoted as saying, "Too many kids were getting hooked too easily." The Platzspitz, a garden spot in the center of Zurich, was devastated. Statues were marred with graffiti. The ground was littered with used syringes and soaked with urine. Citizens avoided the area and the city finally ended its experiment. The park was closed and surrounded by a high fence to keep out the drug addicts and dealers. Plans are now being implemented to renovate the park and restore its original beauty. Zurich has served as a real-life experiment that proves the failure of decriminalization.

We believe that we must change public attitudes toward drugs and focus on prevention and treatment, but we must also maintain the laws making drugs illegal. A goal of prevention is to create an environment that rejects drug use and dealing. Effective prevention involves a comprehensive approach that includes the following components: education, including information about drugs; helping children understand the pressures from friends, family and school that may promote the use of drugs; social-competency skills to assist them in resisting the temptations of drugs; making available intervention (counseling, treatment) to those who have begun to use drugs; promoting positive alternatives to drug use; providing training to those who relate to children and influencing social policies.

Effective prevention efforts also attempt to promote negative attitudes toward drug use by communicating clear, consistent anti-substance-abuse messages through the mass media, within communities and in educational settings. A final important prevention strategy is to enforce stringently the laws against illegal drugs in order to control their availability.

When community prevention efforts are coupled with strong and decisive national leadership, the chances for change are greatly enhanced. Perhaps the most dramatic examples of the effectiveness of these partnerships are the anti–drunk driving and anti-smoking campaigns. These campaigns grew out of public intolerance of problems that not only plagued their communities, but decimated their children. Volunteers, community activists, parents and youth groups organized, developed community prevention strategies and applied unrelenting pressure on public officials, the private sector and the media. These activists were influential in shifting public attitudes. At the same time, Federal as well as state and local officials passed laws and changed public policies to regulate smoking in public areas, limit advertising and increase drunk-driving penalties. The result has been fewer traffic fatalities and a decrease in the social acceptability of drunk driving and smoking.

A study conducted by the New York State Division of Substance Abuse Services in 1990 found that during the preceding 12 years marijuana, cocaine and alcohol use had declined among school-age children. National data show similar trends. Studies of high school seniors conducted over the past decade have shown a dramatic decline in drug use as well. Legalizing drugs now would only send a confused message that could be interpreted as implying that the Government condones their use.

THE COSTS TO SOCIETY

While legalization may appear to be a realistic solution to a very difficult problem, it would be a tremendous mistake. With legalization would come an increase in availability of drugs and an increase in the problems associated with their abuse: the suffering of addicts and their loved ones; the death and loss of thousands of innocent lives; great costs to society, to the health-care system, to employers, and, above all, social, economic and emotional costs to our children.

Instead of legalizing drugs, we must devote massive resources to education and treatment. We must communicate the clear and consistent message that drugs are destructive and will not be tolerated. We must so change public policy and attitudes that every addict who wants treatment can receive it. We must continue to use our resources to enforce the laws against drugs in order to keep drugs out of our communities. Rather than giving up the fight and legalizing drugs, it is crucial that we redouble our efforts to solve the problem.

Periodical Bibliography

The following articles have been selected to supplement the diverse views presented in this chapter. Addresses are provided for periodicals not indexed in the *Readers' Guide to Periodical Literature*, the *Alternative Press Index*, the *Social Sciences Index*, or the *Index to Legal Periodicals and Books*.

Paul Armentano	"The New Reefer Madness," *Liberty*, January 1997.
Joseph A. Califano Jr.	"Legalization of Narcotics: Myths and Reality," *USA Today*, March 1997.
Christian Science Monitor	"Legalization: No Answer," February 8, 1996.
Thomas W. Clark	"Keep Marijuana Illegal—for Teens," *Humanist*, May/June 1997.
James A. Inciardi and Christine A. Saum	"Legalization Madness," *Public Interest*, Spring 1996.
William London	"Will Legalizing Drugs Benefit Public Health?" *Priorities*, vol. 7, no. 2, 1995. Available from the American Council on Science and Health, 1995 Broadway, 2nd Fl., New York, NY 10023-5860.
Eric Schlosser	"More Reefer Madness," *Atlantic Monthly*, April 1997.
Paul B. Stares	"Drug Legalization: Time for a Real Debate," *Brookings Review*, Spring 1996.
Andrew Peyton Thomas	"Marijuana and Mea Culpas," *American Enterprise*, May/June 1997.
Cal Thomas	"The War on Drugs: Declare Defeat and Get Out?" *Conservative Chronicle*, February 14, 1996.
R. Emmett Tyrrell Jr.	"No to Drug Legalization," *American Spectator*, April 1996.
Walter Wink	"Getting Off Drugs: The Legalization Option," *Friends Journal*, February 1996. Available from 1216 Arch St., 2A, Philadelphia, PA 19107-2835.
Mortimer B. Zuckerman	"Great Idea for Ruining Kids," *U.S. News & World Report*, February 24, 1997.

CHAPTER 4

SHOULD MARIJUANA BE LEGALIZED FOR MEDICAL PURPOSES?

CHAPTER PREFACE

In November 1996, California and Arizona had the opportunity to debate the merits of marijuana for medical purposes when the issue was presented to voters in the form of statewide ballot propositions. In both states, voters agreed that medical marijuana should be allowed. As of 1998, the Arizona legislature had effectively rescinded the proposition in that state, while law enforcement officials in California have adopted a range of innovative strategies to deal with their new law. All the ramifications of the new law have yet to become clear, but the debate continues about its merit, and other states are watching California's experiment carefully.

Many critics of the new law agree with William J. Bennett, who argues that "nobody denies that marijuana's euphoric qualities would cause individuals to feel good (as would a few shots of Wild Turkey). The question for science is whether marijuana treats disease, not whether it makes people feel giddy." Supporters of medical marijuana, such as conservative Republican and cancer patient Richard Brookhiser, claim more specific benefits than just feeling good. Smoking marijuana, they assert, eases certain kinds of pain, reduces nausea caused by chemotherapy, and restores appetite to AIDS sufferers. "To deal with the resulting nausea [from chemotherapy], I took legal antiemetic drugs, but after a while they didn't work. Then, I turned to pot," Brookhiser says.

Complicating the debate over marijuana for medical purposes is the existence of the drug Marinol, a pill that contains THC, the main active ingredient in marijuana. Those who oppose medical marijuana contend that sufferers should just take Marinol instead of smoking pot. However, some patients who have tried both drugs say that Marinol is not as effective as smoked marijuana and complain about the pill's side effects. Advocates of medical marijuana also argue that the federal government is being inconsistent by claiming that there is no medical benefit to marijuana while endorsing a drug containing the primary active ingredient in pot. Indeed, the Food and Drug Administration (FDA) has approved Marinol for medical use while continuing to prohibit marijuana for medicinal purposes.

The debate over Marinol and the experiment with medical marijuana in California are among the issues examined in the following chapter concerning the use of marijuana as a medicine and its ramifications for the war on drugs.

"I have seen hundreds of AIDS and cancer patients who are losing weight derive almost immediate relief from smoking marijuana, even after other weight-gain treatments . . . have failed."

MARIJUANA REDUCES SUFFERING FOR SOME ILLNESSES

Part I: Richard Brookhiser, Part II: Marcus Conant

In the following two-part viewpoint, a cancer patient who uses marijuana and a doctor who encourages his patients to use the drug address the typical objections to the use of marijuana for medical purposes. In Part I, cancer patient Richard Brookhiser, a senior editor of the conservative *National Review*, responds to the contention that marijuana has not been sufficiently tested by noting that the government simply has not allowed the necessary testing. Brookhiser also rejects the argument that allowing sick people to use marijuana will encourage young people to take the drug. In Part II, Marcus Conant maintains that nothing else works as well as marijuana in relieving nausea and stimulating appetite in AIDS and cancer patients. Conant, a teacher at the University of California, San Francisco, has treated more than five thousand HIV-positive patients.

As you read, consider the following questions:

1. According to Brookhiser, why is smoking marijuana better than taking the THC pill Marinol?
2. Why does Conant suggest that government arrests of doctors who prescribe marijuana is a First Amendment issue?

I

In November 1996, the voters of California and Arizona made it legal to use marijuana as a medicine. The Clinton administration said these actions were too rash. But for me, they came in the wrong states and four years too late. In 1992, my doctor in New York told me that I had metastasized testicular cancer, which required chemotherapy. To deal with the resulting nausea, I took legal antiemetic drugs, but after a while they didn't work. Then, I turned to pot.

THE MUNCHIES

I hadn't smoked marijuana since college—I had quit because I didn't like the smoke, the high or the jokes of potheads. But I went back to it because the craving to eat that pot induces in the healthy ("the munchies") fights nausea in the sick. None of my doctors or nurses discouraged me from smoking dope. They had all treated patients who successfully used marijuana to keep food down. It worked for me, too.

Cancer patients are not the only sick people who get relief from smoking pot. Marijuana has reportedly restored the appetite of AIDS patients, arrested the deterioration of the eyes of glaucoma sufferers and relieved the symptoms of chronic migraines, epilepsy and multiple sclerosis. But anyone with a disease who turns to pot must break the federal law that makes marijuana illegal in all circumstances.

THREE MISTAKEN OBJECTIONS

Opponents of medical marijuana typically make three arguments, all of them mistaken.

The first is that THC, the main active ingredient in the drug, is legally available in a pill (marketed as Marinol). But the pill, besides being expensive, seems to cause higher levels of anxiety and depression. Since I was trying to combat vomiting, I didn't think a pill was the smart way to go.

The second argument is that marijuana hasn't been thoroughly tested. But that's mainly because the government gives scientists the runaround. Dr. Donald Abrams, an AIDS researcher, has been trying to get marijuana from the National Institute on Drug Abuse. All he gets is the brushoff. If it supplies Abrams, NIDA says, it might be overwhelmed by requests from other researchers. Can't have that—then there might be some research.

The third objection is that legalizing marijuana for the sick would set a bad example for children targeted by drug pushers.

But how? A bald-headed cancer patient lounging by an IV pole is not an image of cool.

Attorney General Janet Reno is threatening to prosecute doctors who prescribe marijuana to patients. For an administration composed, in part, of former recreational drug users (including President "Didn't Inhale"), the decision to harass doctors who use these same drugs to treat the sick is unseemly. Supporting this policy is also unseemly for my fellow Republicans, whose aim is supposed to be reforming Big Government.

In a few months, I will finish my fifth year free from cancer. God forbid that any policy makers in Washington should go through what I did in 1992. But inevitably some will—and will turn to marijuana for relief. They should extend that same liberty to their fellow citizens.

II

Anyone who has ever smoked marijuana will tell you he gets hungry afterward. That kind of anecdotal evidence led doctors and patients to experiment with marijuana as a treatment for extreme nausea, or wasting syndrome. I have seen hundreds of AIDS and cancer patients who are losing weight derive almost immediate relief from smoking marijuana, even after other weight-gain treatments—such as hormone treatments or feeding tubes—have failed. But it's not just individuals who have recognized the medicinal benefits of marijuana. No less an authority than the FDA has approved the use of Marinol, a drug that contains the active ingredient in marijuana.

The problem with Marinol is that it doesn't always work as well as smoking marijuana. Either you take too little, or 45 minutes later you fall asleep. Even though insurance will pay for Marinol—which costs about $200 a month—some patients spend their own money, and risk breaking the law, for the more effective marijuana. That's fairly good evidence that smoking the drug is superior to taking it orally.

NOT WHOLESALE LEGALIZATION

How would we keep patients from giving their prescribed marijuana to friends? The same way we keep people from abusing other prescription drugs: by making patients understand the dangers of giving medication to other people. A physician who prescribes marijuana without the proper diagnoses should be held up to peer review and punished. There are drugs available at the local pharmacy—Valium, Xanax, Percodan—that are far more mood-altering than marijuana. They aren't widely abused.

It's not important that a few zealots advocate the wholesale legalization of marijuana. The federal government can't craft policy based on what a few irrational people say. This is a democracy, and what the people of California voted for was to make marijuana available for medical use for seriously ill people.

For skeptics, a study devised at San Francisco General Hospital would test the benefits of smoking marijuana once and for all. It, too, was endorsed by the FDA—but the federal government won't provide the marijuana for the study. Washington recently offered to fund a $1 million review of literature on medical marijuana, but it refuses to allow a clinical trial, which is what's really needed.

GOVERNMENT SHOULD NOT INTERFERE

When citizens even speak up in favor of legalizing marijuana for medicinal use, as happened in 1996 in California and Arizona, the government tries to stop them. Gen. Barry McCaffrey and the Justice Department have threatened to revoke the prescription-drug licenses of doctors who prescribe marijuana. This is a truly dangerous step. The government has no place in the examination room. Our society has long felt that certain relationships require privileged communication, such as those between a priest and a parishioner or a lawyer and a client. If a patient wants to discuss marijuana, I don't want to have the responsibility of reporting him, and I have to feel comfortable that the patient will not report me. This is a First Amendment issue of freedom of speech between doctor and patient.

Perhaps the most persuasive argument for medicinal marijuana I've encountered came when the California Assembly was debating a medical-marijuana bill. One GOP assemblyman said he had had a great deal of trouble with the issue. But when a relative was dying a few years before, the family had used marijuana to help her nausea. That story helped the bill pass. Wouldn't it be awful if people changed their minds only after someone close to them had died?

> "There is no scientific evidence to suggest that marijuana—particularly when ingested by smoking—is beneficial treating illnesses."

MARIJUANA PROVIDES NO MEDICAL BENEFITS

Dan Quayle

In the following viewpoint, former vice president Dan Quayle criticizes the 1996 initiatives that legalized medical marijuana in California and Arizona. These initiatives were not sponsored out of compassion for sufferers of disease, according to Quayle. In his view, they were designed as a stealthy first step toward the legalization of all drugs for all citizens. Quayle, who writes frequently on drug issues in his nationally syndicated column, argues that there is no medical evidence demonstrating the usefulness of marijuana.

As you read, consider the following questions:

1. According to Quayle, what is the definition of a Schedule I drug?
2. What groups are united in their opposition to medical marijuana, according to the author?
3. What evidence does Quayle cite to support his view that the medical marijuana initiatives are part of a larger drug legalization strategy?

Reprinted from Dan Quayle, "Drug Initiatives Have Too Many Loopholes," *Conservative Chronicle*, December 4, 1996, by permission of Creators Syndicate.

S everal years ago, when then-Surgeon General Joycelyn Elders suggested that we consider legalizing drugs, she was widely (and properly) criticized. While most of the country continued to talk about the importance of fighting drugs, proponents of drug legalization were busy developing a strategy to accomplish their goal. Their first step: legalizing marijuana for medicinal use.

Now those involved in the drug war are confronted with myriad challenges. Teen drug use has skyrocketed in recent years, with marijuana use doubling from 1994 to 1995. And now, a new issue has appeared. On Nov. 5, 1996, when voters in California approved Prop. 215 and those in Arizona gave their nod to Prop. 200, supporters of drug legalization won two important battles.

RIDDLED WITH LOOPHOLES

On the surface, these initiatives seem to make sense. They were presented to voters as an act of compassion for those suffering from diseases such as cancer, AIDS, glaucoma and multiple sclerosis. Advocates of Prop. 215 and Prop. 200 argued that people suffering from these diseases should have the right to use marijuana—and, in Arizona's case, a variety of other drugs—to help them cope with their diseases. Pretty straightforward, right? A simple act of compassion?

Well, not exactly.

California's Prop. 215, which passed 55 percent to 45 percent and is now state law, legalized the use of marijuana for medicinal purposes. But the measure was so poorly written (perhaps intentionally) that it is riddled with loopholes and essentially legalized the use of marijuana in California.

Arizona's Prop. 200, which passed 64 percent to 36 percent, was a bit more complicated. Cloaked in the garb of waging a tougher war on drugs, it legalized all Schedule I drugs for medicinal purposes. For those unfamiliar with the term, Schedule I drugs are those having a high potential for abuse, not currently accepted for medicinal use and unable to be prescribed. Marijuana, heroin, LSD and methamphetamines are all Schedule I drugs, which also carry the designation "not safe or effective for humans." [Proposition 200 was overturned by the Arizona state legislature in 1996.]

NOT SUPPORTED BY DOCTORS

There are numerous problems associated with both of these initiatives, but two main issues are paramount. First, to put it bluntly, there is no scientific evidence that marijuana, or any other Schedule I drug, is safe or effective. That is why both propositions were opposed by virtually every doctors' organization in the country. Among others, the American Medical Association, American Cancer Society, National Multiple Sclerosis Association and American Academy of Ophthalmology all opposed these measures.

EXCUSES TO GET HIGH

All the "medical uses" for marijuana, including asthma, seizures, multiple sclerosis, muscle spasms, etc., are really just excuses to get high. Some users may be under the delusion they are being helped, but pot users typically smoke for the THC while still taking the standard medications for their disease. . . .

Using marijuana for illness would be like a physician prescribing moldy bread (containing penicillin) for pneumonia or suggesting cigarette smoking for stress or weight loss. Prescribing pot for any medical condition is totally irresponsible. Some doctors do and are either naïve about the damage marijuana causes or perhaps are users themselves.

Paul Leithart, *New American*, October 13, 1997.

Doctors were not the ones advocating the use of marijuana for medicinal purposes. Indeed, virtually all of the money used to promote the measures came from longtime advocates of drug legalization.

The propositions also skirted the FDA approval process. I have often been critical of the FDA's method of approving drugs, and I will no doubt continue to be so, but there is no scientific evidence to suggest that marijuana—particularly when ingested by smoking—is beneficial treating illnesses. As a result, the FDA has not sanctioned it.

During the [presidential] campaign [of 1996], Republicans were highly critical of Clinton's waging of the drug war. The passage of Props. 215 and 200 give him an excellent opportunity to make amends and begin his second term on the right foot.

BAD MEDICINE

General Barry McCaffrey, the national drug czar, was a strident critic of both initiatives and worked to defeat them. Writing about the California measure, he noted that it was "bad medicine and bad for children. As politics, the bill is dishonest. The attempt to exploit human suffering is shameful. California voters need to know that marijuana is neither safe nor effective."

. . . Clinton should immediately follow the lead of his drug czar. This is an issue where the American people need strong leadership from the president, and before the end of [1996], Clinton should travel to Arizona and California, explain why he agrees with Gen. McCaffrey and make it clear that the use or possession of marijuana is still a crime under federal law.

The champions of Props. 215 and 200 are already taking their successful strategy to other states. All Americans, from the president on down, need to be ready to help convey the message that marijuana is a dangerous drug that is not appropriate for medicinal use.

| "Redefining marijuana as medicine makes people less likely to automatically agree that it is an unmitigated evil."

LEGALIZING MARIJUANA AS MEDICINE IS A POSITIVE CHANGE IN THE WAR ON DRUGS

Nick Gillespie

Nick Gillespie, a senior editor of *Reason* magazine, believes that the passage of medical marijuana initiatives in California and Arizona in 1996 challenges the extreme antidrug tone of the current war on drugs. Since marijuana will no longer be seen simplistically as a purely evil substance, national leaders of the war on drugs will be forced to adopt new strategies and acknowledge the misleading nature of their rhetoric, according to Gillespie. He believes that the legalization of marijuana as medicine may well lead to a wider rejection of the war on drugs.

As you read, consider the following questions:

1. What evidence does Gillespie provide in support of his view that voters in California and Arizona were not voting for the legalization of marijuana for general use?
2. According to the author, why do groups advocating the legalization of marijuana fear a backlash from the recent initiatives?
3. In Gillespie's view, how does the drug Marinol prove the benefit of marijuana as medicine?

Reprinted, with permission, from Nick Gillespie, "Prescription Drugs," in the February 1997 issue of *Reason* magazine. Copyright 1997 by the Reason Foundation, 3415 S. Sepulveda Blvd., Suite 400, Los Angeles, CA 90034.

In the run-up to November's [1996] elections, opponents of California's Proposition 215 and Arizona's Proposition 200—both of which allow doctors to recommend or prescribe currently illegal drugs—drove home one basic point: These ballot initiatives were, in the words of Clinton drug czar Barry McCaffrey, "a stalking horse for legalization." California's initiative, Orange County Sheriff Brad Gates warned, "wouldn't just legalize marijuana for medical use—it would legalize marijuana, period, with absolutely no controls on quality, or dosage, or who can get it." State Rep. Paul Mortenson (R-Mesa) told the *Arizona Republic*, "The message from Proposition 200 is, Do drugs, so what?" "What we have here," pronounced California Attorney General Dan Lundgren, "is a law flying under false colors."

In the end, however, what opponents had was a failure to convince. Even the vast majority of voters in both states who oppose drug legalization remained unpersuaded. Indeed, the final tallies weren't even close: Fifty-six percent of Californians favored Proposition 215, with 44 percent opposed. Arizona's Proposition 200 scored an even more lopsided win, 65 percent against 35 percent.

Sympathy for the Suffering

The medical-use initiatives carried the day due not to any nascent push for widescale legalization but to the huge reservoir of sympathy people have for desperately ill patients and chronic pain sufferers. Pre-election polls commissioned by Arizonans for Drug Policy Reform, the group pushing Prop. 200, found less than a quarter of state residents favored legalization. Election exit polls on the initiative, however, showed overwhelming support in every demographic group, including Republicans, conservatives, and Dole voters.

In the wake of such success—and national polls suggesting receptiveness to the idea—the medical-use movement is sure to spread across the country. Californians for Medical Rights, one of the main proponents of Prop. 215, has renamed itself Americans for Medical Rights and will lobby for similar measures in other states. And Rep. Barney Frank (D-Mass.), who in 1995 introduced a medical marijuana bill in Congress, says he will introduce new legislation similar to the California initiative.

These votes represent the most significant shift in drug policy in recent years—not because they allow medical use as a covert means of legalization, but because, in the words of the chief organizer of the Arizona initiative, they "make the debate on legalization possible for the first time." They do so by challenging the drug war's axiomatic assumption that "illegal" or "illicit" drugs are demonic substances that offer no possible benefits to society. As one tenet of the drug war's underlying philosophy is opened to debate, it seems likely a more expansive reconsideration of the whole enterprise may be in the offing. . . .

California's Compassionate Use Act of 1996 largely grew out of the experience of illegal but semi-tolerated "buyers' clubs" that provide marijuana to chemotherapy, AIDS, glaucoma, and chronic pain patients. . . .

The measure closely resembles laws twice passed by the state legislature but vetoed by Gov. Pete Wilson. It allows patients to possess, grow, and consume pot on a doctor's "recommendation" that "the person's health would benefit from the use of marijuana" in treating terminal illnesses such as cancer, "chronic pain," or—and this is what gave opponents fits—"any other illness for which marijuana provides relief." Prop. 215 also stipulates that a patient's "primary caregiver"—defined as "the individual designated by the person...who has consistently assumed responsibility for the housing, health, or safety of that person"—is not subject to criminal sanctions. Doctors recommending use would similarly be exempt from punishment or other sorts of retribution, such as the lifting of state medical licenses. . . .

Arizona's Prop. 200 promises a broader impact than California's initiative. It enables doctors to prescribe any Schedule I drug—a category that includes marijuana, heroin, LSD, MDMA, and other illegal substances—if they can cite research that "supports" a medical application and they obtain a concurring written opinion from another doctor. Those prescriptions would provide a valid, legal defense against drug possession or use charges. The act also includes a number of criminal justice provisions designed to "medicalize" the drug war: People without valid prescriptions who are convicted of possession or use fewer than three times can't get jail time; state prisoners serving time for nonviolent use or possession—conceivably as many as 1,800 people—are immediately eligible for a parole hearing and possible release. Parolees and newly convicted people will have to attend court-ordered drug treatment, education, and community service. A truth-in-sentencing provision holds that anyone convicted of committing a violent crime while high must serve 100 percent of his sentence.

No Hidden Agenda

Organizers of both efforts remain emphatic that the propositions cover only legitimate, defensible medical use—a position somewhat undercut when Californians for Compassionate Use's Dennis Peron recently told the *New York Times* that "all marijuana use is medical—except for kids." But Bill Zimmerman, head of Californians for Medical Rights, has also stated unambiguously on CNN's *Crossfire* that he is opposed to legalization of drugs and that the law's provisions apply only to patients under the care of certified physicians.

Even proponents who support drug legalization agree on the narrow focus. If anything, says Dale Gieringer, head of the California chapter of the National Organization for the Reform of Marijuana Laws and a co-organizer of the Prop. 215 drive, most legalization advocates fear a backlash and so are particularly keen to build a fire wall between "medicalization" and legalization. California NORML is circulating a guide about Prop. 215 which notes in bold-faced, capital letters: "PROP. 215 IS FOR SERIOUSLY ILL PATIENTS. DO NOT ABUSE IT BY TRYING TO MAKE UP BOGUS MEDICAL EXCUSES. NORML SUPPORTS THE RIGHT OF ADULTS TO USE MARIJUANA RECREATIONALLY, BUT WE DO NOT CONDONE THE ABUSE OF PROP. 215 FOR NON-MEDICAL PURPOSES. NOT ONLY DOES SUCH BEHAVIOR INVITE A PUBLIC BACKLASH, IT IS ILLEGAL AND SUBJECT TO PROSECUTION."

"One thing doctors don't want to do is to take time out of their practice to testify in court," notes Dr. Jeffrey Singer, a Phoenix-area surgeon who was a spokesman for Arizona's Prop. 200. Because prescriptions for Schedule I drugs will be subject to court scrutiny and justification, doctors will have every reason to follow both the letter and spirit of the law, says Singer, an open advocate of drug legalization and donor to libertarian groups. . . .

CONFLICTING DRUG LAWS

More difficult questions revolve around the interaction of the new statutes with federal drug laws. Under federal law, it remains illegal to manufacture, use, possess, or distribute any Schedule I drugs, including marijuana. So even patients following doctors' orders—and complying with state laws—are violating federal law. The position of doctors is more complicated still. While doctors are already prohibited from prescribing Schedule I drugs, the U.S. Drug Enforcement Administration also licenses physicians to prescribe controlled substances such as morphine. The DEA carefully tracks the use of such drugs and exercises powerful oversight in that area. It is not clear if the feds will respond to doctors who prescribe or recommend Schedule I drugs by revoking their authority to prescribe controlled substances. Indeed, it is not even clear how the DEA will learn that doctors are prescribing marijuana or other Schedule I drugs, since those prescriptions will not be filled by pharmacists. . . .

At least in the short run, the DEA seems to be adopting a wait-and-see posture, ready to spring on any evidence of increased use among children and other groups as a way to move public opinion to support a federal crackdown. McCaffrey's office has announced plans to "actively collect data—i.e., drug related accident rates, teen pregnancy, work absences, hospital emergency cases, and the like—which will indicate the consequences of the referenda." It will be interesting to see what that discovery process turns up, especially since McCaffrey's conclusion already seems firmly in place: "A hoax has been perpetrated and will be exposed," he wrote after passage of Props. 200 and 215. "By our judgment, increased drug abuse in every category will be the inevitable result of the referenda."

MARIJUANA IS DOCTOR APPROVED

Marijuana prohibition depends on the drug's demonization. In the name of sustaining the drug war, we are taught that marijuana is lethal, carcinogenic and addictive. While marijuana has its risks, especially for children, none of this is true. Neither is it true that marijuana has no accepted medical use; in 1991, almost half the oncologists who answered a Harvard Medical School survey said they would prescribe marijuana for relief of chemotherapy side effects were it legal, and most had already recommended it to their patients.

Dan Baum, *Nation*, December 2, 1996.

In fact, very little is inevitable in the wake of the propositions. No one—opponent or proponent—knows for sure what will happen. In California, thousands of "registered" marijuana users already receive their pot from buyers' clubs. And, says NORML's Gieringer, there are already "scores" of doctors publicly "recommending" pot to patients. How much will medical-use rates change in the face of Prop. 215? Will more doctors get with the program? "There's no way to know," he says.

Singer, the Phoenix-area surgeon, says that although the Arizona law allows doctors to prescribe any Schedule I drug, "the most typical application will be marijuana for cancer patients and spinal-cord injury patients"—uses understood and seemingly accepted by the public. Will public opinion shift if doctors prescribe more controversial substances for less-sympathetic patients? How will voters react when the first parolees leave Arizona state prisons?

Similarly, it's unclear how recreational drug-use rates will change—or even whether such fluctuations can be tied to the initiatives. Nor can we know whether the possibility of a legal defense for possession and use of illegal drugs will discourage state and local cops from pursuing all such cases.

A New Conversation

Following the passage of Props. 200 and 215, perhaps only this much is certain: A new conversation about drug policy is taking place, one that actually requires state and federal governments to enter into dialogue with citizens. "Just say no" has been answered with "Tell us why." It is not clear that the government will be able to hold up its end of the discussion.

In his official statement lamenting the new state laws, McCaffrey sputtered, "We had support from former Presidents Ford, Carter, and Bush"—as if a trinity of one-term ex-chief executives would somehow provide a boost to any cause. The statement reflects a flustered mindset, one that has not had to work hard in the past to win arguments: "Doctors will not recommend pot when there are clearly better treatments. Most parents do not want their kids smoking dope. The problem is, there will be a small group of doctors recommending marijuana to people."

As Americans for Medical Rights and other groups push initiatives in other states, the conversation about the medical use of currently illegal drugs is bound to continue. Frank says the California and Arizona initiatives "give some real oomph" to the medical-use debate. "They are another argument for changing federal law," he says. Although he concedes such a change is unlikely to unfold quickly, he suggests that Congress will take note of public opinion.

Nor, despite what opponents claim, is there any reason to assume that medical-use laws lead inexorably to legalization. Indeed, the "medicalization" of drug laws can be seen as simply shifting control from the criminal justice system to a more insidious, paternalistic authority (the Maricopa County, Arizona, Libertarian Party urged a "no" vote on Prop. 200 for similar reasons). While people may be willing to expand the current pharmacopoeia [stock of allowable drugs], they are not necessarily signing on to the idea that individuals should have the right to decide what drugs they can take. Just as drug warriors must explain themselves to a skeptical public, so too must legalizers.

The potential connection between medical use and legalization is, in fact, a fairly subtle one. McCaffrey has suggested, "There could not be a worse message to young people than the provisions of these referenda. Just when the nation is trying its hardest to educate teenagers not to use psychoactive drugs, now they are being told that 'marijuana and other drugs are good, they are medicine.'" On one level, such an equation is absurd: People—including teenagers—don't take drugs recreationally because they are certified as "good" medicine. If they did, we could expect a run on any number of drugs, ranging from Kaopectate to penicillin. At the same time, redefining marijuana as medicine makes people less likely to automatically agree that it is an unmitigated evil.

The real contribution of medical marijuana to the larger debate on legalization is that it may well put the lie to official claims about drugs. Lungren, for instance, has said that smoking or eating marijuana has no beneficial medical effect (even as he allows that Marinol, a prescription version of THC, the main active ingredient in marijuana, has some value). At the very least, recent events will focus more critical scrutiny on government statements. When McCaffrey presents his evidence of the "inevitable result of the referenda," he will have to work to convince his audience.

FAILURE TO COMPROMISE

Yale Law School Professor Steven B. Duke suggests that if the public sees more and more people using marijuana medically and testifying to its value, they may rethink their position on it. "There might be a recognition as well that the government is lying in other areas of drug policy, too," says Duke, co-author of *America's Longest War: Rethinking Our Tragic Crusade Against Drugs.* "Among prohibitionists, there's a sense that if you give an inch, you lose everything. That's certainly the case with [opponents] of medical marijuana." Ironically, the failure to compromise on a relatively noncontroversial topic such as medical marijuana could open the door to a much broader rejection of the drug war.

It is in this sense that the initiatives have, as Arizona's John Sperling puts it, made the "debate on legalization possible." What shape it will take and what ends it will achieve are far from certain. Judging from poll data, there is currently little support for legalization. But as the passage of Props. 200 and 215 forces prohibitionists to justify their policies, and the country's experience with the open medical use of illegal substances gets underway, that debate should prove to be one full of possibilities.

"Not only is marijuana not medicine,
its use is especially contraindicated
for many of the people who will be
encouraged to use it."

LEGALIZING MARIJUANA AS MEDICINE IS DETRIMENTAL TO THE WAR ON DRUGS

William J. Bennett and John P. Walters

Supporters of the medical marijuana initiatives passed by voters in California and Arizona in the Fall of 1996 argued that marijuana provides a unique kind of relief to those who suffer from AIDS and cancer. William J. Bennett and John P. Walters contend that, contrary to the claims of these medical marijuana advocates, marijuana has little or no medical value. Bennett and Walters argue that the real goal of the backers of these initiatives is the eventual legalization of all currently illegal drugs. Bennett is the former director of the Office of National Drug Control Policy, while Walters is former deputy director of that office. Together with John J. DiIulio Jr., they are coauthors of *Body Count: Moral Poverty—and How to Win America's War Against Crime and Drugs*.

As you read, consider the following questions:

1. Why do Bennett and Walters claim that smoking marijuana may actually harm cancer patients more than help them?
2. According to Bennett and Walters, who funded the medical marijuana initiatives and why?
3. How might federal authorities prevent doctors from prescribing marijuana, according to the authors?

Reprinted, with permission, from William J. Bennett and John P. Walters, "Medical Reefer Madness," *Weekly Standard*, December 9, 1996.

As if cops didn't have enough problems, the Drug Enforcement Administration is up against a new obstacle. A DEA press release paints this scene:

> A patrol officer encounters a 16-year-old female accompanied by an 18-year-old male. Both state he is her "primary caregiver." Both are found to be in possession of marijuana and he readily admits providing it to her on the "recommendation" of a doctor at a local clinic for relief of "nausea."

Make all the players in this little drama Californians, and the patrol officer is powerless to intervene. Thanks to a ballot initiative legalizing the "medicinal" use of marijuana, California is now virtually unable to restrict marijuana use by people of any age. Proposition 215, which passed with little fanfare in November 1996, also allows cultivation and possession by individuals who are not sick, provided they claim, as did the young man above, to be the "primary caregiver" of someone using marijuana to combat "any . . . illness for which marijuana provides relief."

NO MEDICAL UTILITY

The problem is that marijuana has never been scientifically demonstrated to provide "relief" from any medical condition—at least no more relief than other licensed drugs that are much less prone to abuse. This critical point was obscured in a campaign whose small band of wealthy out-of-state backers outspent the opponents of Prop. 215 seventy-five to one.

In fact, the notion that marijuana has demonstrated medical utility has been rejected by the American Medical Association, the National Multiple Sclerosis Society, the American Glaucoma Society, the American Academy of Ophthalmology, and the American Cancer Society.

Pot activists rhapsodize about marijuana's usefulness in "treating" glaucoma. But medical researchers believe otherwise. Dr. George L. Spaeth, first president of the American Glaucoma Society and director of the Glaucoma Service at the Wills Eye Hospital in Philadelphia, has "not found any documentary evidence which indicates that a single patient has had his or her natural history of the disease altered by smoking marijuana." Dr. M. Bruce Shields, president of the American Glaucoma Society and chairman of the department of ophthalmology at Yale University, expresses "reservations" about the use of cannabinoids to fight glaucoma, particularly since there are "many drugs that are much better than the marijuana analogues and that have significantly fewer side effects." Dr. Richard P. Mills, vice chair of the University of Washington department of ophthalmology, explains that glaucoma sufferers already have access to six "families" of glaucoma medication, at least one of which controls the disease in almost every patient. Dr. Keith Green, director of ophthalmology research at the Medical College of Georgia, has studied the use of marijuana and its active ingredient, THC, to treat glaucoma and finds "no evidence that marijuana use prevents the progression of visual loss."

NOT EFFECTIVE FOR NAUSEA

Proponents also cite marijuana's alleged utility in controlling nausea. Yet Dr. David S. Ettinger, associate director of the Johns Hopkins Oncology Center, writes, "There is no indication that marijuana is effective in treating nausea and vomiting resulting from radiation. . . . No legitimate studies have been conducted which make such conclusions." As for nausea resulting from chemotherapy, the American Cancer Society states that "other . . . drugs have been shown to be more useful than marijuana or synthetic THC as 'first-line therapy' for nausea and vomiting caused by anti-cancer drugs."

Marijuana boosters often cite a 1988 study showing that smoking marijuana helped 44 of 56 cancer patients who suffered from nausea. But this study lacked a control group, and 87 percent of the subjects experienced toxic side effects. Moreover, although the authors admit that "oral THC is an effective treatment for chemotherapy-induced [vomiting]," only 29 percent of the subjects who benefited from smoking marijuana had already tried oral THC. In other words, patients were asked to use marijuana before the scientifically approved remedies had been exhausted. The entire debate may be irrelevant, however. Notes Dr. Richard J. Gralla, director of the Ochsner Cancer Institute in New Orleans, "There has been a revolution in the treatment and prevention of nausea since 1988."

Unfortunately, not only is marijuana not medicine, its use is especially contraindicated for many of the people who will be encouraged to use it by California's new law. Cancer patients' immune systems are weakened by radiation and chemotherapy, leaving them susceptible to infection, and marijuana use further compromises their immune systems. That's in addition to the drug's well-known harmful effects on brain cells, lungs, and circulation.

Yet, despite the evidence, and after 24 years of trying and failing, the pro-pot side carried the day. The California initiative passed with 55 percent of the vote, capping a 24-year effort by NORML and other groups to gain public sanction for widespread marijuana use on the basis of the drug's supposed "medicinal" qualities.

Why this sudden success? The difference is that in 1996 the potheads had access to that mother's milk of politics—money. Campaign finance laws place a $2,000 ceiling on individual contributions in national races, but the ballot initiative process has no such limitations. Foremost among the financiers and businessmen whose backing secured passage of Prop. 215 was George Soros.

Based in London and New York, Soros is a currency trader and investor with a fortune estimated by *Forbes* at $2.5 billion. He is also sugardaddy to the drug legalization movement, committing, by his own reckoning, more than $15 million to various groups since 1991, including $980,000 to the California initiative and the similar initiative that passed in 1996 in Arizona. [Arizona's Proposition 200 has since been overturned by the state legislature.] Groups funded by Soros contributed at least another $300,000, and Soros solicited at least one contribution of $200,000. In all, the organization that flacked Prop. 215, Californians for Medical Rights, raised $2 million for the campaign, including $750,000 in the first 19 days of October alone. In contrast, the opposition, Citizens for a Drug-Free California, spent a total of $26,000 and aired no paid TV commercials.

A STEALTH STRATEGY

Soros and company are pursuing a stealth strategy designed to conceal their real agenda: legalizing all drugs. In a 1994 interview with *Rolling Stone* magazine, the president of Soros's Open Society Institute, Aryeh Neier, explained that Soros gave the pro-legalization Drug Policy Foundation a "set of suggestions to follow if they wanted his assistance: Come up with an approach that emphasizes 'treatment and humanitarian endeavors,' [and] . . . target a few winnable issues, like medical marijuana and the repeal of mandatory minimum [sentences]."

Soros was joined in the campaign by Arizona businessman John G. Sperling, who gave $630,000 to the California and Arizona initiatives. Sperling is adamant that doctors should be allowed to prescribe all drugs, including heroin and LSD: "I don't think that there should be any substance outside the pharmacopoeia [allowable stock of drugs]. Sperling is less clear on exactly why. When asked for studies that show the utility of these drugs, he cited anecdotal evidence: "You go from anecdote to anecdote to anecdote, and there are so many people who say their lives have been changed for the better." Of course, nobody denies that marijuana's euphoric qualities would cause individuals to feel good (as would a few shots of Wild Turkey). The question for science is whether marijuana treats disease, not whether it makes people feel giddy.

Sperling disagrees. "The drug problem," he says, is "a public health problem, primarily. It only becomes a crime when you put people in prison for it." People who deny this are "either intellectually dishonest, stupid, or both, and that goes for most members of Congress, the president, and the man who wanted to be president."

NO EVIDENCE NEEDED

Sperling is not alone. Former U.S. senator Dennis DeConcini served as the Arizona campaign's unofficial poster child, appearing in commercials and on TV news opposite drug czar Barry R. McCaffrey. Like others we interviewed, DeConcini was unable to cite a single scientific study showing marijuana's medical effectiveness. Not that this bothers him: "To me it's irrelevant whether you have a study or not," he says, so long as the law has "compassion" and requires a doctor's prescription (as it does in Arizona, but not in California).

Chris Britt. Reprinted by permission of Copley News Service.

Passage of the two initiatives notwithstanding, use of marijuana for nonmedicinal purposes remains a crime in California and Arizona. Unfortunately, as the DEA anticipated, the change in state law has weakened local law enforcement, and federal agents cannot be expected to take up the slack. There are 7,000 state and local narcotics officers in California, more than ten times the number of DEA agents in the sate. And the federal agents concentrate on large traffickers, not users.

Even so, the feds may have a role in containing the damage from Prop. 215 and its counterpart in Arizona. Under a "public interest" provision of the Controlled Substances Act, the DEA can revoke the "registration" license every physician needs in order to store, dispense, or prescribe controlled substances. Historically, the DEA has worked in tandem with state authorities, but nothing in the law prevents it from moving unilaterally against the small number of pro-pot physicians who are likely to recommend marijuana for their patients. If the Clinton administration is serious about halting the rise in drug use among the young, its DEA will prepare to use this power.

SNAKE OIL

DEA chief Thomas A. Constantine, for one, is clear-eyed on the issue. He likens medicinal marijuana to "snake oil," the harmful, all-purpose curatives sold by hucksters at the turn of the century. The analogy is apt.

Little more than diluted morphine, the likes of "Coats Cure" and the "Richie Cure" were eventually regulated out of existence under the 1906 Pure Food and Drug Act. This law was passed at the urging of Progressive reformers after the wild success of the snake-oil scam had brought on America's first great drug epidemic. Progressives were occasionally criticized for worshipping at the altar of science, a claim unlikely to be levelled against the proponents of medical marijuana.

"Whatever the potential relief pot
may offer seriously ill patients, we
know that smoked marijuana
contains carcinogens and that it
poses a real and present danger to
our youth."

MARIJUANA IS TOO DANGEROUS TO LEGALIZE FOR MEDICAL PURPOSES

Joseph A. Califano Jr.

Joseph A. Califano Jr. argues in the following viewpoint that the approval of medical marijuana without adequate proof of its usefulness will only encourage the misconception that marijuana is not harmful to one's health. Califano believes that the current enthusiasm for medical marijuana is similar to the enthusiasm for the cancer drug laetrile in the 1970s. Though there was initially much anecdotal evidence suggesting that laetrile cured cancer, the proper scientific tests eventually revealed that the drug was useless. Califano calls for a cautious approach to medical marijuana in order to ensure that such a mistake is not made again. Califano, who was secretary of health, education, and welfare from 1977 to 1979, is president of the National Center on Addiction and Substance Abuse at Columbia University.

As you read, consider the following questions:

1. Why are some doctors advocating the smoking of marijuana, according to the author?
2. According to Califano, why is marijuana use particularly harmful to young people?
3. In Califano's view, how strong is the link between marijuana use and cocaine use?

Reprinted, by permission of the author, from Joseph A. Califano Jr., "Medical Marijuana and the Lesson of Laetrile," *Washington Post National Weekly Edition*, February 24, 1997.

The current rush to medical marijuana is reminiscent of the furor over laetrile in the mid- to late 1970s.

Remember laetrile? That was the concoction of crushed apricot pits with cyanide that was touted as a cancer cure. More than half the states legalized its use, and many judges responded to pleas of frantic cancer victims to make laetrile available to them. I was secretary of Health, Education and Welfare at the time.

FOOL'S GOLD

Though scores of patients and some physicians claimed laetrile purged their malignant cells when everything else failed, by all the science at the time it was a fool's gold. Yet, in a bow to the desperation of terminally ill cancer victims, I asked Arthur Upton, director of the National Cancer Institute, to review claims of cure. Doctors and clinics in Mexico and the United States refused to turn over their patient records to the institute. Nevertheless, pressure for the government to back off opposition to laetrile built, and several members of Congress demanded that I order the Food and Drug Administration to approve it for physician prescription.

Responding to these pressures, Upton wanted to run tests in humans. FDA head Donald Kennedy considered such a course unethical because there was no evidence that laetrile had any medicinal value, and patients in the trial would be required to forgo other treatment that might offer some long-shot possibility. Kennedy also was concerned about trying laetrile on humans without any prior animal tests, thus abandoning well-established procedures for assessing the safety and effectiveness of a new drug.

Upton disagreed, as long as the individuals being tested knew the score. He saw laetrile use as a public health problem: "At least 50,000 cancer patients in the U.S. are now taking laetrile," he said. "We have an obligation to demonstrate that laetrile is either useful or useless so people will know."

I shared Kennedy's reluctance to launch a trial so long as there was no indication that laetrile could cure cancer. But use of laetrile increased. In 1980 the National Cancer Institute and the FDA worked out a protocol to test laetrile, even though there was still no evidence that it had any medical value. In justifying this decision, one of the doctors involved, Charles Moertel of the Mayo Clinic, said, "Laetrile has assumed proportions that no other quack medicine has assumed before."

The tests demonstrated that laetrile was indeed worthless, and cancer patients stopped using it.

With the fervor of those who believed in laetrile, proponents of the medical use of marijuana claim it relieves nausea and sparks appetite in cancer and AIDS patients, and that it eases the pain of muscle spasms and glaucoma. Phillip Lee, assistant secretary for health in the Department of Health and Human Services, says that "there is no scientifically sound evidence that smoked marijuana is medically superior to currently available therapies, including an oral prescription medication containing the active ingredient in marijuana."

THE DANGERS OF MARIJUANA

Marijuana is an unstable mixture of over 400 chemicals. When smoked, it produces 2,000 chemicals, many of which are cancer-causing substances. It can be addictive, adversely affects the immune system, causes respiratory diseases, can lead to mental disorders, impairs coordination and judgment, and is known to increase the incidence of leukemia and low birth weight among the newborn children of abusers.

Robert Maginnis, *World & I*, December 1996.

But the furor continues, and the National Institutes of Health are now working with the FDA to "resolve questions about the alleged therapeutic value of [smoked] marijuana." That's not fast enough for some, including the editor of the *New England Journal of Medicine* and several doctors, who urge that traditional procedures to determine efficacy and safety be bypassed and marijuana be made available immediately to seriously ill patients who want it. Drug legalization advocates are stepping up their pressure on states to legalize medical marijuana, much as 27 states did with laetrile in the 1970s. In the fall of 1996, two states passed referenda legalizing medical use of illegal drugs—marijuana in California; marijuana, heroin, LSD and other drugs in Arizona.

UNDERSTANDABLE DESPERATION

The desperation of cancer and AIDS patients is as understandable today as the pleas of the cancer victims for laetrile were in the 1970s. In the 1990s, Americans seem even more prone to let seriously ill patients take any medicine (and perhaps any action, including suicide) that they wish. This view is buttressed by a growing resentment of government interference, especially in the doctor-patient relationship.

But with marijuana now as with laetrile then, it is worth

counting to 10. Let the NIH and FDA run smoked marijuana through the tests that have for the most part avoided tragedies here that have beset other nations (such as Britain with thalidomide babies) that moved too fast to release untested drugs.

With marijuana there is more reason to move cautiously. Legalization for medical purposes is likely to make marijuana more readily accessible and acceptable to teens. Whatever the potential relief pot may offer seriously ill patients, we know that smoked marijuana contains carcinogens and that it poses a real and present danger to our youth. Smoking marijuana can savage short-term memory, impair ability to maintain attention and motor skills, and inhibit emotional, intellectual and physical development—when teens are learning in school and experiencing rapid development. With the sharp rise in marijuana use among 12- to 17-year-olds since 1991, we had better be ready with a stepped-up public health campaign to keep our kids off pot if we are going to send them signals that it's great stuff for their sick parents and grandparents.

A SERIOUS LOOK

We also know that teens who smoke pot are 85 times likelier to use drugs such as cocaine than those who have never done so. That relationship may be only statistical, but when the surgeon general found a nine- to 10-times-greater likelihood of lung cancer among cigarette smokers, and the Framingham heart study found a two to four times greater likelihood of heart disease among individuals with high cholesterol, Congress and the National Institutes of Health invested billions in biomedical research. Any serious look at marijuana demands the same kind of investment. If we had made it years ago, we might have been able to put the present emotional and political debate over medical marijuana to rest right now—with scientific knowledge and medical experience.

| "The oft-repeated lie that marijuana is some kind of deadly poison leads people—especially young people—to suspect all suggestions that drugs may be dangerous."

MARIJUANA IS NOT TOO DANGEROUS TO LEGALIZE FOR MEDICAL PURPOSES

Virginia I. Postrel

In the following viewpoint, Virginia I. Postrel contends that the passage of medical marijuana initiatives demonstrates that marijuana is not the dangerous drug portrayed in messages from the government's war on drugs. On the contrary, Postrel claims that many average Americans, including some formerly skeptical conservatives, concede that marijuana is beneficial for some medical conditions. According to Postrel, the widespread public acceptance of medical marijuana challenges much of the war on drugs rhetoric on marijuana, which she sees as misleading and excessively negative. Postrel is editor of *Reason*, a monthly libertarian magazine.

As you read, consider the following questions:

1. What is Postrel's main evidence in support of her claim that marijuana is a relatively harmless drug?
2. How will the federal government prevent doctors from prescribing marijuana, according to Postrel?
3. According to the author, why has so little research involving marijuana's effects on people been done so far?

When California and Arizona voters gave substantial majorities to the proposition that sick people ought to be allowed to use marijuana (and, in Arizona, other illegal drugs) if it might ease their suffering, the reaction in Washington was predictable: utter horror. Propositions 215 and 200 struck not only at the heart of drug war propaganda but also at the most sensitive assumptions underlying the regulatory state.

For drug warriors, Propositions 215 and 200 are terrifying because these laws recognize that marijuana is not especially dangerous. "We have a problem," said Health and Human Services Secretary Donna Shalala at the Clinton administration's anti-initiative press conference. "Increasing numbers of Americans believe that marijuana is not harmful." Indeed.

NOT A DEADLY POISON

Like the once-common insistence that steroids do not help athletes bulk up, the oft-repeated lie that marijuana is some kind of deadly poison leads people—especially young people—to suspect all suggestions that drugs may be dangerous. It's hardly surprising that drug use has turned up among the most propagandized generation in history, or that almost all the upswing is accounted for by casual pot smoking. You don't have to smoke marijuana yourself, or even have a very wide circle of friends, to find plenty of anecdotal evidence that the drug is neither particularly hazardous to health nor the gateway to drug-abuse hell. If she doubts this commonsensical observation, Shalala could ask the president or vice president, among numerous other administration officials with marijuana smoking in their past. Or she could consult mountains of scientific research, much of it aimed at proving the dangers of dope.

As Lester Grinspoon and James B. Bakalar wrote in a 1995 editorial in the *Journal of the American Medical Association*: "One of marihuana's greatest advantages as a medicine is its remarkable safety. It has little effect on major physiological functions. There is no known case of a lethal overdose; on the basis of animal models, the ratio of lethal to effective dose is estimated as 40,000 to 1. . . . It is true that we do not have studies controlled according to the standards required by the FDA[Food and Drug Administration]—chiefly because legal, bureaucratic, and financial obstacles are constantly put in the way. The situation is ironical, since so much research has been done on marihuana, often in unsuccessful attempts to prove its dangerous and addictive character, that we know more about it than about most prescription drugs.". . .

Just as anti-gay conservatives are far more threatened by stable, bourgeois same-sex couples (who want to get married!) than by anonymous bathhouse sex or exhibitionists parading in leather jockstraps, nothing would undermine the official line on drugs more than lots of respectable, otherwise law-abiding people admitting that they smoke marijuana without ruining their lives. Very few responsible recreational users, however, are likely to risk the legal consequences of coming out of the closet.

The medical marijuana initiatives bypass that problem. They introduce a prospect even more threatening to the status quo: What kind of mean-spirited person, after all, would deny sick people relief? As Jim Christie reported in *Reason*, even Pat Buchanan sympathizes with patients who need pot, as did Newt Gingrich back in 1981. Yet if thousands—or even hundreds—of average Americans suddenly start admitting in public that they smoke marijuana to relieve various illnesses, the demonization of the drug can't be sustained.

THREATENING DOCTORS

The Clinton administration is trying mightily not to appear to be attacking physicians. When asked about what they planned to do to deter doctors from recommending marijuana, Shalala and her law-enforcement colleagues—Attorney General Janet Reno and drug czar Barry McCaffrey—dodged desperately. "This isn't about physicians," said Shalala. "This is about truck drivers. It's about workers in federal buildings. It's about teachers." In other words, it's about doctors *and their patients*.

And the administration is quite assuredly threatening doctors. "We are going to take very, very serious action against them," Drug Enforcement Administration head Thomas Constantine told the *New York Times*. Reno, meanwhile, urges local authorities to "make arrests and prosecute." Remember, too, that what's at stake is merely *recommending* marijuana—free speech, in other words, between physicians and patients. The administration that began its first term by repealing the so-called gag rule prohibiting federally funded clinics from advising patients about abortions is starting its second by trying to impose a gag rule in cases where federal money isn't even involved.

THE APPROVAL PROCESS

In their attempts to manipulate the public by misusing the language, administration officials have decided to wrap themselves in science. Instead of defending the criminal law—which, for the most part, doesn't even fall under their jurisdiction—they are relying on pharmaceutical regulation to save them.

"We have a consensus in this country and *national* law that establishes a standard for drugs that are used in California and in New York. The NIH [National Institutes of Health] and the FDA are the core of that approval process," said Shalala at the December 30, 1996, press conference. "If it starts falling apart and every state legislature can suddenly approve a drug—not based on any scientific fact—we are undermining the basic health and scientific standard by which this country has established the most extraordinary quality of health care. . . . What's at stake are our youngsters, but just as important, the scientific base for our entire health care system."

HOME-GROWN MOVEMENTS

Opponents are painting Props 215 and 200 as a "stealth" campaign by drug legalizers, financed by out-of-state billionaires. Admittedly, these initiatives wouldn't have gone far without the deep pockets of a half-dozen wealthy businessmen, a couple of whom have supported marijuana decriminalization. But neither ballot measure could have happened without home-grown movements for reform. Like the AIDS movement, the fight for medical marijuana is driven by the suffering of tens of thousands of patients, who've risked arrest and jail time in pursuit of the relief that smoking it affords them. The willingness of business leaders to sign on to the California and Arizona referendums reflects the degree to which this struggle has crossed over to the mainstream.

Sarah Ferguson, *Nation*, January 6, 1997.

This statement was designed to confuse both the journalists in the room and the public at large. For starters, the National Institutes of Health ordinarily have no role in approving drugs. They fund biomedical research, some of which leads to new pharmaceuticals. Most new drugs come not from the government but from private companies, entities that apparently don't exist in Shalala's mental universe. Nor is it clear that U.S. pharmaceutical innovation—much less the "entire health care system," which includes unregulated and highly innovative and successful medical procedures—depends on the FDA.

FOLK REMEDIES

Second, not all biologically active substances fall under Shalala's precious approval process. Some "medicines" are not pharmaceuticals but folk wisdom, often eventually backed by experimental science. If I tell you to put ice or cold water on a burn or eat chicken soup and drink hot tea for a cold, I do not need FDA approval. More analogous—given the product's ordinary use—is the old, and in my experience highly effective, Southern folk remedy of putting a paste of tobacco on bee stings. Suggesting that a plant might relieve your symptoms is not the same as prescribing a commercial pharmaceutical. If marijuana had never been made illegal, using it medically as well as recreationally might require no more FDA approval than drinking herbal tea. And since marijuana isn't patentable, no pharmaceutical company would invest in FDA testing, even if it were legal.

Since it isn't legal, Shalala's "approval process" is not just the FDA's normal hoops—as bad as they are. While there is little doubt that smoking marijuana can relieve glaucoma, chemotherapy-induced nausea, and AIDS-related wasting, it would indeed be nice to have more solid scientific research on the subject. But it's essentially impossible to do efficacy testing on a substance whose very possession is a crime.

No Ongoing Studies

That's where the NIH comes in. You can't just, as a scientific matter, decide to investigate whether marijuana might relieve nausea or migraines. If you want to do your research legally, the DEA and National Institute on Drug Abuse will have to approve—and recent history suggests they won't. (Plus, researching the possible medicinal benefits of evil, illicit, politically incorrect substances is not exactly the way to win friends, grants, or tenure.) As a result, there are no ongoing studies. That Shalala, McCaffrey, and Janet Reno spent a press conference pretending otherwise just shows the Clinton administration's endless ability to twist the facts to suit its political spin.

The Arizona and California propositions don't just subvert the drug war by threatening to expose its propaganda. They attack the favorite argument for big, technocratic government: "health and safety." They dare to suggest that health is, for the most part, an individual, private matter; that safety depends on how each person weighs relative dangers; and that knowledge about both is not the sole possession of centralized bureaucrats. The initiatives explode the most beloved premises of paternalistic Progressivism. No wonder the Clintonistas are going crazy. This isn't a battle they can afford to lose.

PERIODICAL BIBLIOGRAPHY

The following articles have been selected to supplement the diverse views presented in this chapter. Addresses are provided for periodicals not indexed in the *Readers' Guide to Periodical Literature*, the *Alternative Press Index*, the *Social Sciences Index*, or the *Index to Legal Periodicals and Books*.

Dan Baum	"California's Separate Peace," *Rolling Stone*, October 30, 1997.
Dan Baum	"Rx Marijuana," *Nation*, December 2, 1996.
Joseph A. Califano Jr.	"Devious Attempts to Legalize Drugs," *Washington Post National Weekly Edition*, December 9–15, 1996. Available from 1150 15th St. NW, Washington, DC 20071.
Stephen Chapman	"The Drug Warriors vs. Medical Marijuana," *Conservative Chronicle*, January 15, 1997. Available from PO Box 11297, Des Moines, IA 50340-1297.
Consumer Reports	"Marijuana as Medicine: How Strong Is the Science?" May 1997.
Sarah Ferguson	"The Battle for Medical Marijuana," *Nation*, January 6, 1997.
Lester Grinspoon and James B. Bakalar	"Marihuana as Medicine: A Plea for Reconsideration," *Journal of the American Medical Association*, June 21, 1995. Available from 515 N. State St., Chicago, IL 60610.
Hendrik Hertzberg	"The Pot Perplex," *New Yorker*, January 6, 1997.
Jerome P. Kassirer	"Federal Foolishness and Marijuana," *New England Journal of Medicine*, January 30, 1997. Available from 10 Shattuck St., Boston, MA 02115-6094.
Clarence Page	"Reefer Madness: Lift Ban on Medical Marijuana," *Liberal Opinion*, January 13, 1997.
Michael Pollan	"Living with Medical Marijuana," *New York Times Magazine*, July 20, 1997.
Adam J. Smith	"Pot of Trouble," *Reason*, May 1997.
Arnold Trebach and Joseph A. Califano Jr.	"Medical Marijuana," *World & I*, March 1997. Available from 3600 New York Ave. NE, Washington, DC 20002.

CHAPTER 5

WHAT NEW INITIATIVES MIGHT IMPACT THE WAR ON DRUGS?

Chapter Preface

There have been a number of creative initiatives in the war on drugs in recent years, innovations that attempt to break the gridlock felt on certain fronts. Some of these measures have proven controversial, such as the needle exchange program, designed to save the lives of intravenous drug users by preventing the spread of HIV. Another controversial program has been the use of National Guard troops along the Mexican border to try to catch drug smugglers. The potential problems of this initiative were highlighted by the accidental shooting death of a Texas teenager in 1997 by Guard troops who mistakenly suspected him of smuggling drugs.

One of the most innovative new strategies in the war on drugs is the widening use of drug courts to deal with nonviolent drug offenders. Drug courts provide an alternative to the usual outcome of drug arrests—release or jail time—by promoting a strictly regulated rehabilitation strategy for drug offenders. In drug courts, judges and lawyers attempt to work together to achieve a positive result for each offender. According to Judge Jeffrey Tauber, who presides over a drug court in Oakland, California, these courts involve "the development of an ongoing, working relationship between the judge and the offender and the use of both positive and negative incentives to encourage compliance." The use of positive incentives is an obvious departure from courts that rely heavily on incarceration. The offender who completes treatment and rehabilitative measures on schedule receives verbal praise and applause in the court setting as well as a reduction both in fines and the length of the rehabilitation program. In another departure, prosecuting attorneys openly endorse rehabilitative measures in place of long jail sentences. Critics of this approach see it as "coddling" criminals. Moreover, convincing long-term statistics proving its efficacy are not yet in. But participants in drug courts frequently feel this option provides offenders with a fighting chance to avoid further drug abuse problems.

Drug courts are just one of many recent innovations in the ongoing war on drugs. The following viewpoints look at this and other new approaches in the effort to prevent drug abuse in the United States.

"*[We are]* making prevention of drug use among our youth priority number one."

THE WAR ON DRUGS SHOULD FOCUS ON TEENAGERS

Barry R. McCaffrey

Barry R. McCaffrey is the director of the White House Office of National Drug Control Policy. The following viewpoint is excerpted from a speech he delivered to members of Congress in 1996. McCaffrey argues that the recent increase in teenage drug use, including tobacco and alcohol, calls for a renewed emphasis on prevention by the federal government. The keys to discouraging drug use by teenagers, he maintains, are education and the influence of authority figures. McCaffrey contends that focusing on teenagers, who are at a responsive age, will be the best way to prevent adult abuse of harmful drugs.

As you read, consider the following questions:

1. According to McCaffrey, what percentage of teenagers does not use illegal drugs?
2. What does the author mean by the term "gateway drug" with reference to tobacco use by teenagers?
3. In McCaffrey's opinion, what laws are needed in response to the problem of teenage drinking and driving?

Reprinted from Barry R. McCaffrey, "Prevention Programs Work," address to the Senate Judiciary Committee, September 4, 1996.

G lamorization of drugs, alcohol, and tobacco condones adolescent use. The glamorization of drugs has not been limited to television and film portrayals. It also occurs in videos and
the lyrics of popular music, advertising and marketing (i.e. fashion's heroin chic look), comedy, the Internet, and merchandis-
ing where items like jewelry, T-shirts, temporary tattoos, candy,
and soft drinks are among the products that promote drug use.
The promotion of drugs permeates every facet of a child's life.
The Budweiser frogs and Joe Camel are very familiar cartoon
characters for our children. This inundation of pro-alcohol, tobacco, and other drug messages occurs at a time when new
technology and techniques enable media to form more dramatic, multi-sensory, and powerful images than ever before.
PSAs [public service announcements] and other antidrug messages have demonstrated the ability to influence attitudes towards drugs among today's youth. Prevention messages must be
repeated with adequate frequency and in appropriate venues so
that they can counter pro-drug messages.

INADEQUATE PREVENTION AND EDUCATION PROGRAMS

Some people have suggested that the programs designed to educate our children about the dangers of drugs are not doing a
good job and are not cost effective. The Office of National Drug
Control Policy absolutely disagrees with this assessment. Despite
rising numbers of young people using drugs, the 1995 National
Household Survey on Drug Abuse (NHSDA) shows the overwhelming majority of our children, 89.1 percent, were not current users of illegal drugs. Less than one percent used cocaine.
Clearly, most kids are filtering everything they hear about drugs
and are reaching an intelligent conclusion: "Using drugs is not
good for my health." Unfortunately, it is also clear that we lack
sufficient rigorous studies demonstrating the effectiveness of
different prevention programs. We need such information so
that we can justify to the American people the expenditure of
counterdrug resources. . . .

THE TOP PRIORITY

[We are] making prevention of drug use among our youth priority number one. The first goal of the 1996 National Drug
Control Strategy targets substance abuse by young Americans.

Monitoring the Future's 22 years of tracking youth attitudes
and drug usage establishes that we can influence youth attitudes
towards drugs and cause them to modify their behavior. . . .

We must prevent drug use on the part of the demographic

bulge formed by children of the baby boom generation. There are 68 million Americans under the age of 18 and 39 million under the age of 10. Ten years from now if the younger group abuses drugs at the same rate as today's teens, drug use will increase by alarming proportions. If drug use rises at the same rate it has for the past five years, by the year 2000, 1.4 million high school seniors will be using illegal drugs on a monthly basis. We cannot afford this outcome. Nor do we want new addicts to swell the ranks of adult hard-core drug users (3.6 million) who are the human wreckage of our nation's extensive drug use in previous decades.

The president's 1997 counterdrug budget affirms this commitment to reduce drug use by requesting more than $1 billion to support drug education that targets youth attitudes. Two major initiatives include:

Safe and Drug-Free Schools and Communities Program ($540 million requested). This program will fund drug and violence prevention activities for more than 40 million students in 97 percent of the nation's school districts.

SAMHSA's [Substance Abuse and Mental Health Services Administration] Prevention Programs ($371 million requested). These programs include community partnership projects that support parents' coalitions, schools, religious institutions, public housing authorities, business, organized labor, industry, government, and professionals in developing and maintaining long-term prevention strategies.

PREVENTING TOBACCO USE

Despite a decline in adult smoking, the use of tobacco products is on the rise among American youth. In 1995, more than a third of high school seniors smoked cigarettes, a greater number than at any time since the 1970s. The threat to our children's health is tremendous. The vast majority of smokers (over 80 percent) start smoking before age 18. Approximately 4.5 million children under 18 smoke cigarettes or use smokeless tobacco in the United States. Every day, nearly 3,000 more children become regular smokers; almost 1,000 of these youngsters will have their lives shortened by tobacco-related diseases, the leading cause of preventable death in this country.

Is tobacco a "gateway drug"? While we do not at this time have any scientific evidence of a direct cause and effect relationship between the use of tobacco and other drugs, a strong statistical correlation exists. Youths aged 12–17 who smoke are about 8 times more likely to use illicit drugs and 11 times more likely to drink heavily than nonsmoking youths. A study conducted in 1994 by Columbia University Center on Substance Abuse and Addiction found that 83 percent of those who used cocaine identified smoking cigarettes as gateway behavior. Finally, we know that nicotine is an addictive substance that causes neuro-chemical reactions similar to those produced by cocaine, heroin, and amphetamines.

1996 Worldwide copyright by Cartoonews International Syndicate. Used by permission.

We don't want our children smoking cigarettes or using other tobacco products. That's why the President announced an initiative to reduce tobacco use by children. This initiative will reduce children's access to tobacco products, reduce the appeal of tobacco products to young people, and educate children about the hazards of tobacco.

PREVENTING ALCOHOL USE

Alcohol is the number one illegal drug problem among young people. It is the drug abused most frequently by our children, and is responsible for 35 percent of the highway deaths among our youth. In the '40s and '50s, young people often took their first drink at the age of 13 or 14. Today, they frequently start at age 12. The 1996 NHSDA shows the mean age of first use of alcohol declining since 1990; in other words, younger and younger children are beginning to drink. Three to four million teenagers are now alcoholics. Our youth are consuming 35 percent of all wine coolers sold in the United States and more than a billion cans of beer.

The Administration is encouraging states to enact zero tolerance laws designed to reduce drinking and driving among young people. These laws establish that effectively any measurable amount of alcohol in the blood, breath, or urine of a driver under age 21 would constitute an illegal, per se, offense. Most of these laws also provide for the immediate suspension of drivers' licenses for individuals under the age of 21 who exceed the blood alcohol concentration limit. These measures (already passed in 37 states), together with the minimum age drinking law, are saving young lives today. . . .

THE FIRST LINE OF DEFENSE

The problem of increasing drug use among young people is not going to be solved by Washington alone. Combined efforts will be needed from individual Americans, communities, and organizations concerned with our children's well-being. . . .

Our first line of defense against drug use among youth must be the parents, teachers, coaches, ministers, and counselors running youth-oriented organizations. These people have the greatest influence on our children. Youngsters and adolescents listen most to those they know love and respect them. It is critical that the 50 million Americans who used drugs in their youth but have now rejected illegal drugs participate in this national prevention effort. We are unlikely to reverse these negative trends if all Americans do not participate in what must be a national effort. We also will need the active support and attention of the news media to educate all Americans about the nature of the drug abuse threat we face.

We must ensure that parents are aware of the dangers drugs pose so that they will speak to their children about drugs. We should arm parents with the information they need. Children can be misled easily by myth, rumor, and the false notion that drugs are glamorous. For our children's sake, we need to act today. By doing so, we can reduce the number of addicted adults who will cause enormous damage to themselves and our society tomorrow.

"The implicit message sent to kids and the general public is that legal drugs are not as harmful as illegal drugs."

ANTIDRUG CAMPAIGNS SHOULD ALSO TARGET TOBACCO AND ALCOHOL

Norman Solomon

In the following viewpoint, Norman Solomon contends that some antidrug ad campaigns ignore the abuse of alcohol and tobacco. Solomon maintains that media and government silence on this issue has sent the message that smoking and drinking are ultimately not that harmful. However, he contends, tobacco and alcohol are in fact the most damaging drugs in society. For this reason, Solomon argues that antidrug campaigns should also target tobacco and alcohol abuse. Solomon is a syndicated columnist and coauthor (with Jeff Cohen) of Through the Media Looking Glass: Decoding Bias and Blather in the News.

As you read, consider the following questions:

1. What has been omitted from the $2 billion ad campaign of the Partnership for a Drug-Free America, according to the author?
2. According to Solomon, how many more people die per year from tobacco and alcohol use than from drug use?
3. In the author's view, what is the real reason ABC does not include alcohol and tobacco in its news reports dealing with drug abuse?

Reprinted from Norman Solomon, "The Partnership for a Candor-Free America," Liberal Opinion Week, March 17, 1997, by permission of Creators Syndicate.

The most famous anti-drug commercial in history—a frying egg and a somber warning, "This is your brain on drugs"— is badly in need of a sequel.

Our new spot opens with a wide-angle shot of a press conference featuring the president of ABC Television. Also in the picture are speakers from the Partnership for a Drug-Free America, plus federal officials in charge of education, health and drug policy.

"This is your nation's leadership on drugs," the announcer intones. "A more sanctimonious and hypocritical bunch you couldn't imagine."

With the help of computer graphics, the dignitaries slowly morph into upscale partygoers. Some are smoking cigarettes, others are sipping cocktails—and all have large checks spilling from their pockets.

"On March 4, 1997, these men and women gathered in Washington to launch yet another 'anti-drug' campaign," the script goes on. "But they continued to tiptoe around the most damaging drugs in our society. As a practical matter, they're flunkies for the multibillion-dollar interests behind cigarettes and alcohol."

TOBACCO AND ALCOHOL ARE IGNORED

You might think that such a public-service ad would be unfair. But consider these facts:

• The U.S. government is providing half the funds for a new $350 million media campaign against drugs. But the advertising drive—which depends on matching donations from media companies—will give short shrift to cigarettes and alcohol.

• In March 1997, the ABC television and radio networks engaged in a "March Against Drugs" programming blitz with little to say about smoking and drinking.

• During the past 10 years, the Partnership for a Drug-Free America has produced $2 billion worth of ads. None of them have said an ill word about tobacco or alcohol.

The Partnership depends on free air time and print space. "By far, ABC has contributed more media time and space than any other company," the organization declares. "Our tremendous success over the past decade is a direct reflection of their belief in our cause."

ABC'S MARCH AGAINST DRUGS

Now, after joining itself at the hip with the Partnership and like-minded federal officials, ABC News is in no position to let the chips fall where they may.

"ABC's March Against Drugs"—which has enlisted such key shows as "Good Morning America" and "World News Tonight"— would more aptly be named "ABC's March Against Journalism."

In a letter to ABC, several drug-policy groups blasted the Partnership: "By excluding any mention of alcohol and tobacco, the implicit message sent to kids and the general public is that legal drugs are not as harmful as illegal drugs." Yet, in the United States, "over 500,000 people die each year from alcohol and tobacco— 35 times the number of deaths from all illegal drugs combined."

MATURE ACTIVITIES

Mike Males, a sociologist who authored *The Scapegoat Generation*, points out that federal authorities concentrate on badmouthing under-age use of tobacco and alcohol—thereby enhancing the image of smoking and drinking as "mature" activities.

"Instead of teaming up with political and private drug-war interests to scapegoat young people," Males comments, "ABC and other media would do a far greater public service to investigate at arm's length why the war on drugs is such a monumental failure."

THE MOST DESTRUCTIVE DRUG

People tend to minimize the occasional teen-age beer blast as kids being kids. But, as drug policy scholar Mark Kleiman of the University of California at Los Angeles notes, alcohol is the drug on which kids "are most likely to get pregnant, commit crimes, get in fights or drive recklessly." No one wants to acknowledge that it's more dangerous for teen-agers to get drunk than to smoke marijuana. But it is.

Stephen Chapman, *Conservative Chronicle*, September 4, 1996.

Clearly, finger-wagging techniques don't work. Extensive research—including the U.S. Education Department's recent evaluation of D.A.R.E. programs—proves that "just say no" messages are not effective in reducing drug use among children and adolescents.

SELECTIVE COVERAGE

Because the Partnership for a Drug-Free America has refused to utter a word against cigarettes or alcohol, news media have found it easier to downplay those major threats to public health. The current anti-drug effort by ABC is a case in point.

When ABC faxed me a dozen pages about its March 1997 special news reports with "anti-drug themes," the only targeted drugs were marijuana, heroin and "sniffing inhalants." The selective coverage will, no doubt, gratify the beer marketers and conglomerates with tobacco holdings that pour huge ad revenues into ABC's coffers.

Talk about addiction! From the network suites of ABC to the Partnership for a Drug-Free America to officialdom in Washington, movers and shakers are hobbled by dependency on this nation's legal drug sellers—the alcohol, tobacco and pharmaceutical firms that are all too happy to focus anti-drug ire elsewhere.

Take a look around. This is your country. This is your country on drugs.

| "Harm reduction offers an opportunity for communities to affect public health and drug policy and repair some of the damage wrought by the war on drugs."

THE HARM REDUCTION APPROACH SHOULD REPLACE THE WAR ON DRUGS

Lisa Moore

In the following viewpoint, Lisa Moore promotes an approach to drug abuse called harm reduction, which puts the health and well-being of drug users at a high priority. Moore argues that the war on drugs, both historically and in the present day, has involved considerable racial bias and has had little success in helping drug users overcome their problems. The harm reduction approach, she concludes, is more humane than government policies based on a philosophy of punishment. Moore is an assistant professor in the Department of Health Education at San Francisco State University.

As you read, consider the following questions:

1. What early stereotype concerned black men, cocaine, and rape, according to Moore?
2. According to the author, what is the "zero tolerance" law enforcement approach concerning search and seizure tactics?
3. In Moore's view, how do syringe exchange programs reflect the harm reduction approach?

Reprinted from Lisa Moore, "In Harm's Way," Crossroads, November 1995, by permission of Crossroads.

The history of people of color and drugs are inextricably linked. In the United States, images of people of color using or selling drugs have been used to fuel propaganda supporting both the present day war on drugs and earlier attempts to suppress human rights. These images belie the reality that the majority of drug users are white. These images also hide the roles that whites, including highly ranked government officials, have in the import and distribution of illicit drugs and how this market has been linked to U.S. foreign policy. While the government promotes drug wars, not drug solutions, often the real efforts of communities of color and their allies to minimize the decimation caused by drug use and abuse are ignored. Harm reduction offers an opportunity for communities to affect public health and drug policy and repair some of the damage wrought by the war on drugs. For people of color in particular, harm reduction offers an alternative to repression and incarceration, and must be part of efforts to organize and politicize communities.

While drugs cause unmistakable harm in communities of color, the war on drugs ignores much of the harm while abrogating the civil rights of inner city residents and scapegoating people victimized by decades of discrimination and social neglect. The history of drugs and drug policy in the United States has always been racialized and that racialization was used to support repressive policies and measures. For example, an early drug czar, Dr. Hamilton Wright, in 1910, issued the "Report on the International Opium Commission," in which he asserted that Blacks on cocaine had superhuman strength and that cocaine prompted Black men to rape white women. These claims induced Southern sheriffs to change the caliber of bullets in order to stop "unstoppable" Blacks on drugs. The claim that Rodney King was uncontrollable due to his alleged use of PCP evoked these fears and exemplified the turn of the century lynchings justified by drug myths.

EARLIER DRUG WARS

Likewise, the Chinese Exclusion Act was, in part, justified by racist concerns about Asian opium smokers and male Asian involvement with white women. Marijuana smoking was also said to drive Mexican Americans to crime and to acts of depravity. Harry Anslinger, who was the director of the Federal Bureau of Narcotics from 1930 to 1962, continued this war on people of color while fighting his drug war. Some of his favorite targets were jazz musicians and one of his political triumphs was in making marijuana smoking a felony. Anslinger was a close colleague of Joseph McCarthy and supplied the senator with morphine, ostensibly to protect him from communist blackmailers.

These early drug wars were, in large part, motivated by desires to control people of color, communists, musicians and others who were "undermining the fiber of U.S. life." Drug policy also has a long legacy intermingling with foreign policy. Our government, while decrying the effects of drugs on Americans and urging citizens to "Just Say No," has a long history of using drugs as part of foreign diplomacy. Drugs have been one of the many currencies of foreign policy, as evidenced in part by the interface of drugs with immigration policies at the turn of the century, the CIA's utilization of opium distribution networks during the Vietnam war, and Oliver North's drugs for guns Iran-Contra scam. North and his colleagues were accused of directly involving themselves in the drug trade while, ironically, in order to further the ends of the war on drugs, other military personnel have been sent to countries like Peru, Colombia and Bolivia to eliminate drugs and to put the growers out of business. In the twentieth century, drug policy has served to extend the long arm of U.S. manifest destiny into the Western Hemisphere.

ZERO TOLERANCE FOR DRUG PROBLEMS

Domestically, the most recent war on drugs, begun by Nixon and expanded during the Reagan-Bush administrations, has succeeded in rescinding some basic civil rights such as protection from search and seizure. Zero tolerance laws offer law enforcement officials carte blanche where all inner-city searches are considered legally justifiable. The state has the right to seize properties associated with the commission of drug-related crimes, and the burden of proof that such property was not associated with unlawful activity rests upon the accused person. Drug problems are no longer in the purview of public health. Out drug policy rests on international interdiction and domestic punishment—with no evident decrease in the amount or quality of drugs available on the street.

As a result of this punitive policy, the U.S. leads other nations in incarcerations, particularly of Black and Latino men. In 1995, approximately 70 percent of federal incarcerations are associated with drug-related offenses. While we are building prisons nationwide at a breakneck speed, our society is simultaneously refusing to commit itself to drug prevention and treatment. Of the $4 billion spent annually on the drug war, 75 percent goes to interdiction and law enforcement. Drug prevention moneys and drug treatment slots are becoming harder and harder to find.

Given the history of the drug war in the U.S., the "concern" about the use of drugs and related harms for people of color becomes a thinly veiled mask over stigmatization and social control. Legislators use drug policy as a means to control people of color both here and abroad—not as a means to get people off drugs or to provide meaningful social and economic options to the sale and use of drugs. Our domestic law enforcement is focused on users and petty dealers rather than on large-scale distributors. All these policies raise questions regarding the government's commitment to stopping the use and trade of illicit drugs.

A CONTINUUM OF CARE

Conventional wisdom assumes that drug abuse and addiction are crime problems; in contrast, many harm-reduction advocates see them as public health problems, like heavy drinking or AIDS. Conventional wisdom assumes that drug use and abuse result from bad individual judgment or character; harm-reduction advocates emphasize the ways the social environment shapes these choices. The drug war solution to drug abuse and addiction is to threaten and punish those who use or deal drugs. Harm-reduction strategies, in contrast, would shift resources toward prevention and treatment, and would redefine and expand the scope of both.

Preventive education for harm reduction would seek to inform and influence individual choices, not only to discourage any use of dangerous drugs but also to educate those who will nevertheless experiment with and use drugs, teaching them how to minimize the harm they cause themselves and others—just as designated driver programs help reduce the harm of drinking. Prevention would also demand policies aimed at changing social environments that encourage abuse and addiction, including abusive family settings, peer pressures and joblessness. Treatment for harm reduction would make total abstinence only one goal along a continuum of care that would include many measures of success: more moderate use, safer use, the use of less dangerous drugs, reduction of criminal activity, ability to fulfill family and workplace roles, greater physical and mental health.

Eva Bertram and Kenneth Sharpe, *Nation*, January 6, 1997.

We are fighting a war on drugs that is, in fact, a war on drug users. The drug war is used to justify military interventions both in the inner city and in Third World countries, and produces a drug market with high profits and no quality control in which armed enforcers fight each other for turf. Yet our government continues to produce propaganda attributing the problems associated with drug use solely to people of color. Many people, including some members of communities of color, have been taught that the only solution to the drug problem is repression and incarceration, and that we must rely on the government to take care of the problem. This perspective is ahistorical and patently false.

AIDS AND HARM REDUCTION

In spite of official disinterest, people-of-color communities have a long tradition of self-help with respect to drug use and abuse. Examples such as the acupuncture detoxification clinic at Lincoln Hospital in the Bronx sponsored by the Young Lords in the 1960s, the treatment activities of the Nation of Islam, and the anti-alcohol community empowerment project of Native people at Alkali Lake, illustrate that people try to protect themselves from drugs and from drug-related harms. Racial/ethnic communities nationwide have launched well-publicized efforts and smaller scale but equally powerful attempts to solve the drug problem by using compassion and the power of community over repression and scapegoating.

The AIDS epidemic has made the need for such organizing and empowerment even more pressing than before. Blacks and Latinos are dying from AIDS at rates double their share of the population, and many of these deaths are associated with the sharing of injection drug equipment. Additionally, non-drug-using sexual partners and children of drug users with HIV are disproportionately people of color. While the toll of AIDS increases in drug-using communities of color, people of color are responding to stem the tide of death and suffering.

THE NEEDS OF USERS

Harm reduction, which seeks to acknowledge the humanity of drug users by planning interventions based upon their expressed needs, is hardly new or innovative on many levels. Drug prevention and treatment, including the programs mentioned above, can be considered part of harm reduction. When communities and families do not exile drug-using members, they are engaging in harm reduction. When churches offer support and succor to drug users, they are doing harm reduction. Communities of color have long traditions with activism around drug use and harm reduction. The AIDS epidemic has just intensified this struggle.

AIDS has primarily affected harm reduction by exposing the importance of starting with the needs of both former and active drug users. Again, this is hardly radical. Successful health strategies incorporate definitions and solutions stated by communities impacted by health problems, and do not use intervention methods solely planned by outsiders. Until the AIDS epidemic, the needs of current drug users were considered irrelevant to health planning. The goal was only to get people off drugs, not to teach them how to use drugs more safely. Because AIDS is incurable, now the focus has shifted to address the needs of active users, as defined by them. Needle exchange, education regarding safer injection and the formation of user unions has become part of disease prevention and health activism. And people of color have played leading roles in all of this.

Like anything, the history of participation in harm reduction activities in this country has hardly been seamless. While support for drug prevention and treatment is universal, the issue of safer using has been highly contested in some communities of color. People have fought the establishment of syringe exchange programs, expressing concerns that teaching people how to inject without spreading disease would send out "mixed messages" that promote drug use. Besieged and neglected communities wonder why people are willing to hand out needles while the government is defunding drug treatment programs and basic health services.

THE POWER OF COMMUNITY

The strength of harm reduction, in the face of such opposition, is that it is more than syringe exchange. Although syringe exchange is an important cornerstone and has, at least in the United States, been the focal point of much of the organizing around the issue, its power rests in how it overlaps with community and political organizing and the provision of other services. Syringe exchange does not stand alone and is most effective when conducted in a context of treatment on demand and universal health and medical services. As a result, harm reduction has prompted some coalition work, between syringe exchange activists, active users and AIDS/drug treatment health workers.

Harm reduction is a proactive approach to the problems produced by the use and sale of drugs in communities. It starts with the needs of all stakeholders in the process, especially the needs of drug users. It does not seek to exile people from their communities through stigmatization and incarceration. Harm reduction seeks to use the political voices of people affected by the epidemics of drugs and AIDS to solve the problem. While the government uses the war on drugs as a means to implement draconian social control measures, harm reduction instead seeks to put the control of people's lives back into the hands of their own communities.

The drug war has been a failure. Its successes are measured by prisons built and the numbers of people incarcerated. The drug war has not stopped the HIV epidemic. It has not even reduced the amount of drugs on the street. The drug war has only succeeded in justifying the excesses of domestic law enforcement and international interventions. Harm reduction offers hope, through political change, social change and democracy, in what has become an increasingly hopeless situation. Communities of color continue to desire and to seek out such hope.

"*A kinder and gentler sort of 'community court' that nevertheless manages to be more strict than the traditional approach is revolutionizing the way the courts deal with drug offenders.*"

Courts Should Emphasize Rehabilitation over Punishment

Michael Moline

The concept of drug courts, in which judges and the prosecution focus on rehabilitation rather than punishment, has become one of the most-discussed new initiatives in the war on drugs. In the following viewpoint, Michael Moline examines the innovative tactics of these courts, arguing that this system of immediate punishments and immediate rewards should be adopted around the country. Moline maintains that because drug courts impose rigorous and sustained oversight on offenders, they are stricter than conventional courts and therefore more likely to help drug offenders rehabilitate. Moline is a freelance journalist in San Francisco.

As you read, consider the following questions:

1. According to Moline, what happens to many drug offenders assigned to rehabilitation programs in the conventional courts?
2. In the author's view, what sentencing options other than simple imprisonment are available to drug court judges?
3. What happens to the role of the offender's defense lawyer in the drug court setting, according to Moline?

Reprinted from Michael Moline, "Innovative Drug Courts: Always Tough, Sometimes Tender," *Nolo News*, Summer 1996, by permission of the author.

I magine a criminal proceeding as a sort of group therapy session, with the prosecution and defense conferring on the best form of therapy to offer the accused, and the judge handing out referrals for acupuncture and bouquets of flowers.

The prospect certainly boggled a few minds in the Oakland, Calif., legal establishment a few years back. But these days similar scenes are played out daily in more than a hundred courtrooms across the country, and the federal government is encouraging more jurisdictions to follow suit.

"Three strikes" laws may be the political rage, but a kinder and gentler sort of "community court" that nevertheless manages to be more strict than the traditional approach is revolutionizing the way the courts deal with drug offenders. And its enthusiasts don't plan to stop there.

"There are juvenile drug courts. There are family drug courts. There are courts that have nothing to do with drugs, at least on the surface, that are using the concepts," said Municipal Court Judge Jeffrey Tauber, who helped dream up Oakland's program.

How It Began

The concepts Tauber talks about had their beginnings about six years ago in cities like Miami and Oakland, where the court system was groaning under the burden of drugs and crime. In some places, half of all defendants—sometimes more—were involved with drugs one way or another, studies showed. Some addicts were committing 500 crimes each year to support their habits.

Diversion programs existed to try to steer defendants into drug rehabilitation, but the oversight was too loose. If a defendant failed his drug tests or simply dropped out of rehabilitation, it might be months or even years before the system caught up with him, and often that was when he was rearrested for another crime.

"It's like when you have a puppy," said District Judge William Meyer, who has been experimenting with the drug court concept in Denver. If the puppy isn't immediately punished for soiling the carpet, it won't learn the cause and effect relationship between its behavior and its consequences, he said.

"Well, that's how it is with many offenders. They're just totally clueless. So, a system of immediate consequences and rewards makes a lot of sense. Frankly, it is my experience and other judges' experience that it works well; people do respond to it."

Typically, drug court judges confer with prosecutors, public defenders, probation officers, the police, local drug treatment programs and community leaders in designing programs to suit local needs. Those same officials also discuss individual cases, finding space in treatment centers, poring over drug test results, deciding what to do with backsliders. Some send participants to acupuncturists to ease the withdrawal pains; some run their own rehabilitation and job training.

"Judges don't go out in the streets, but in some ways we're bringing the streets to the court," Tauber said. "We're developing very close connections with communities."

A CONTRACT WITH THE COURT

Many of these programs use some form of contract between the defendant and the court. The defendant agrees to submit to drug rehabilitation, to pay court costs and perhaps restitution. Someone who does well can reduce the length of parole or probation and court costs, and face less frequent drug tests.

But a flunked drug test, or a missed counseling appointment, court date or Narcotics Anonymous meeting, is swiftly noted and punished, thanks to computer links between judges and rehabilitation programs. The offender might be ordered to take more frequent drug arrests, pay additional costs, move into a detox center or even spend a night or two behind bars. Some flunk out entirely and land in prison.

Each participant's progress is measured in open court, before the gaze of fellow offenders. They can see for themselves the fruits of success when a judge leads a round of applause or hands flowers to people graduating from the program; and also of failure, when habitual backsliders are led away in handcuffs.

"It's the theater of the courtroom, where you use the defendants who are doing well to give their testimonials and words of encouragement to people that are still struggling," said Jay Carver, director of the Pretrial Services Agency in Washington, D.C., which operates a drug court. "Families come in. You can see right in front of you how this process begins to reunite families that may have been torn apart by drug abuse. It's pretty neat stuff.". . .

EXPANDING THE CLIENTELE

Many of the programs target first offenders arrested for simple possession. These pretrial diversion programs offer as their ultimate reward for staying clean the chance to avoid a felony record.

Lately, a few jurisdictions have begun experimenting with harder cases. In Oakland in 1995, the program was expanded to include harder-core drug users in Alameda County Superior Court, people with previous arrests or who refused to participate in the diversion program in the lower court. Their participation won't get their felony charges reduced, but they can secure probation instead of prison time for following a program similar to that in the lower court.

THE GOAL OF REHABILITATION

There is a persistent belief in the judicial community that a drug-using offender's failures while under court supervision are willful and deliberate and consequently ought to be dealt with severely. Unfortunately, this belief fails to recognize the compulsive, addictive nature of drug abuse and the court's limited ability to coerce abstinence.

Drug court judges recognize the limitations of coercion as a drug rehabilitation tool and reject the notion that program failure is necessarily the result of willful defiance of judicial authority and therefore something to be punished as a kind of contempt of court. Rather than using coercion, drug court judges use a pragmatic judicial intervention strategy based on the development of an ongoing, working relationship between the judge and the offender and the use of both positive and negative incentives to encourage compliance.

In a drug court, communications between judge and offender are crucial. By increasing the frequency of court hearings as well as the intensity and length of judge-offender contacts, the drug court judge becomes a powerful motivator for the offender's rehabilitation.

A successful drug court requires the judge and staff to work together as a team. The defense attorney takes a step back—both literally and figuratively—to allow the judge to have direct contact with the offender. The prosecuting attorney adopts a conciliatory position. All staff see their job as facilitating the offender's rehabilitation.

Jeffrey Tauber, *Corrections Today*, February 1994.

Previously, just 6 percent of those defendants ever completed drug treatment successfully, according to Deputy Public Defender Shari Schoenberg.

"I don't want to give the impression that we've found the solution, that this is the panacea," she said. "But I think in an age when we have such diminishing resources, we have to start figuring out new ways to handle these cases that make fiscal sense and are socially responsible. I think this is a good start."

"Society is protected too," said Alameda County Superior Court Judge Martin Jenkins, who presided over the expanded drug court in 1995. "Because of the frequency of our progress reports, if people are not making strides toward that, then the probation can be terminated, or jail time imposed, or a state prison commitment can be effected."

VARIATIONS ON THE DRUG COURT MODEL

The Washington program targets mostly people arrested for small-time drug peddling. There, a federal grant is financing a five-year experiment comparing results from traditional probation and rehabilitation to a new, "advanced treatment" program operated in the court complex itself, as well as to a new "sanctions track" that does not force defendants into treatment, but does require periodic drug testing and imposes escalating punishments for failed drug tests and missed court dates.

"Traditionally, judges only talk to defendants through their lawyers," said Carver. "In the drug court model, the lawyers are part of a treatment team. . . . The lawyer is no longer kind of this barrier between the judge and the defendant."

In New York, the drug court model has been applied toward "quality of life" crimes like prostitution and vandalism that plague city dwellers, said John Feinblatt, coordinator of Manhattan's two-year-old Midtown Community Court.

"These courts are much more problem-solving than some of the traditional courts," Feinblatt said. "Courts see some very complicated problems, and those problems aren't checked at the courthouse door. What we're trying to do is attack some of those problems, which means looking beyond the indictment to what's the impact of the crime on the community and what's the reason for some of the crimes being committed."

OTHER BENEFITS

Since the community court opened, he said, prostitution arrests are down by more than 30 percent, and defendants have contributed some $400,000 in community service labor.

Tauber, meanwhile, estimates that the sort of program he ran in Oakland, if applied statewide, might reduce California's prison population of more than 100,000 by 5,000 to 10,000 inmates. And a National Institute of Justice study found that various drug courts have resulted in reductions in recidivism of between 40 and 60 percent.

"How do you measure success?" Schoenberg wonders. "When we have somebody that comes in and says, 'I've been shooting heroin for 25 years and I've been drug-free for the first 90 days of my life,' I consider that a success."

| "Increased emphasis on treatment will reduce drug demand among heavy users only if more of them become motivated to end their abuse. One way to make them as motivated is coercion."

COERCED PARTICIPATION IN TREATMENT PROGRAMS WILL REDUCE DRUG ABUSE

James Q. Wilson

Because drug demand is declining among casual users, James Q. Wilson asserts in the following viewpoint, the focus of the war on drugs should be on heavy users who are responsible for most drug-related crime. Since the majority of these heavy users come into contact with the criminal justice system at some point, Wilson argues, they should be subjected to coerced treatment at that time. He sees this as the most cost-effective approach to reducing the need for narcotics among users. Wilson is the James A. Collins Professor of Management at the University of California at Los Angeles.

As you read, consider the following questions:

1. Why are efforts to reduce drug demand failing, in Wilson's view?
2. What sanctions would the author apply to those parolees or probationers who fail a drug test?
3. According to Wilson, why would drug tests of many probationers and parolees not involve violation of civil liberties?

From James Q. Wilson, "Use Drug Tests to Reduce Demand for Narcotics," *American Enterprise*, May/June 1995. Reprinted with permission of the *American Enterprise*, a Washington, D.C.–based magazine of politics, business, and culture

There is no doubt that drugs, especially crack cocaine, contribute to crime. What divides experts is why. For some, drugs cause crime because they are illegal: people steal in order to afford their fix, or shoot rivals in order to control illegal markets. For others, drugs cause crime because they alter the subjective state of drug users: drug abuse makes people unfit for regular employment and unable to manage their own lives. Whichever view one takes, crime would be less if the demand for drugs were less.

There is some reason to think that drug demand has in fact declined from 1980s peaks, but this drop is confined almost entirely to light or casual users. For cocaine at least, the number of regular users and the amounts they consume have increased dramatically. As a result, the cocaine problem is as bad today as it was 10 years ago in terms of total consumption, and far worse in terms of its concentration among heavy users.

Supply Reduction Failure

Efforts to reduce drug demand by choking off supplies so that prices rise have had little if any effect. The price of cocaine has been declining and its purity has remained high. Given the vast resources pumped into supply reduction, this seems puzzling, but it can be explained by the economics of drug production.

Experts at the RAND Corporation estimate that the price of cocaine in transit to the United States is $17,000 per kilo, but on U.S. streets that same kilo is worth $129,000. That enormous spread means that even if authorities manage to seize 1 out of every 10 kilos shipped (which seems to be about as much as can be hoped for) the street price on the supplies that get through need only be raised by 1.5 percent to make up for the lost shipment.

This has led most experts to conclude that it is more cost effective to invest in treatment programs—if they work. They do work for people who remain in them. The trouble is that many users, especially young ones, are not really seeking a permanent break from the drug. Increased emphasis on treatment will reduce drug demand among heavy users only if more of them become motivated to end their abuse.

The Advantages of Coercion

One way to make them as motivated is coercion. This is neither as organizationally difficult nor as constitutionally dangerous as one might suspect—if we take advantage of the fact that cocaine use has become concentrated among a relatively small population.

Urine tests in jails show that a majority of newly admitted inmates were using drugs within a day or two preceding their confinement. In the course of a year or two, a large fraction of the heavy crack users in this country fall under the supervision of the criminal justice system. For this reason, prison-based drug treatment programs should be expanded. But they have two limits: First, without community-based follow-up, the relapse rate is likely to be high. Second, three-quarters of all supervised offenders are on the streets on probation or parole, not in prison.

Coerced Abstinence

Imagine a program under which drug-using probationers and parolees were subject to frequent (semiweekly, perhaps) drug tests and automatic, but mild, sanctions for missed or "dirty" tests: perhaps two days' confinement for the first failure, escalating with repeated failures over a short period. (Long sentences would be reserved for those who proved incapable of quitting.) This kind of "coerced-abstinence" system has been proposed and employed with some apparent success in various pilot programs but never made routine in a large jurisdiction or even carefully tested with experimental controls.

But if such a program could be made to work on a large scale, the results might be dramatic. Harvard professor Mark Kleiman has suggested that a reduction in total cocaine volume of 40 percent, far exceeding the impact of any other plausible program, would not be out of range. This would shrink not only the crime rates of those tested, but also the violent illicit markets they prop up.

David Boyum, Insight, June 12, 1995.

Several experts, notably Mark Kleiman, Eric Wish, and Robert DuPont, have proposed making probationers and parolees subject to frequent, random drug tests, with modest but increasingly severe sanctions if they fail the test. Given the short time horizon of drug users, "frequent" would mean several times a week and the sanctions (a night or two in jail, a week on an arduous work crew) would have to be promptly imposed.

Waiving Civil Liberties

Because we would be testing persons already under the supervision of the criminal justice system, the civil liberties problem would be much reduced. Probationers and parolees are not subject to the full protection of the constitutional bar on unreasonable searches, and, in some states, have waived such protection as a condition of their release.

We know from studies that coerced participation can improve the chances of successful treatment. Kleiman estimates that the cost of the testing would be about $2,500 per person per year. There would be additional costs for sanctions, but these could be relatively low if punishments were mild but swiftly applied. All of these outlays would be partially offset by a reduction in drug-caused crime and the attendant investigatory and imprisonment costs.

Such a program has been tried on a pilot basis, but never in a large jurisdiction for an extended period. In order for this to be done, probation, parole, and police officers would need to become aggressive about identifying and testing drug-abusing convicts, judges would need to respond crisply to those who failed the tests, and correctional authorities would need to create a graduated set of sanctions. Some of our new drug courts may be able to achieve these things. But the task would not be easy, as it would require our criminal justice system to succeed at some things it has generally not been good at.

Periodical Bibliography

The following articles have been selected to supplement the diverse views presented in this chapter. Addresses are provided for periodicals not indexed in the *Readers' Guide to Periodical Literature*, the *Alternative Press Index*, the *Social Sciences Index*, or the *Index to Legal Periodicals and Books*.

Richard D. Bonnette and Mary Harrison — "Using a Nationwide Ad Campaign to Turn Children Against Drugs," *San Diego Union-Tribune*, July 24, 1997. Available from PO Box 191, San Diego, CA 92119-4106.

William F. Buckley — "How to Camel-flage Failure," *Conservative Chronicle*, September 4, 1996. Available from PO Box 11297, Des Moines, IA 50340-1297.

Mona Charen — "Lines Drawn on Drugs and Tobacco," *Conservative Chronicle*, September 11, 1996.

Glenn Duncan — "Shattered Dreams: The High Cost of America's Addiction," *Salt of the Earth*, January/February 1996. Available from 205 W. Monroe St., Chicago, IL 60606.

Robert L. Maginnis — "Federal Drug War Ignoring Great Ally: Faith-Based Treatment," *Family Research Council Insight*, May 7, 1997. Available from 801 G St. NW, Washington, DC 20001.

Mike Males — "High on Lies: The Phony 'Teen Drug Crisis,'" *Extra!*, September/October 1995.

Mike Males and Faye Docuyanan — "The Return of Reefer Madness," *Progressive*, May 1996.

Ethan A. Nadelmann — "Stop Kidding About Drug-Free Kids," *Los Angeles Times*, January 3, 1997. Available from Reprints, Times Mirror Square, Los Angeles, CA 90053.

Marsha Rosenbaum — "Lessons in Harm Reduction," *Drug Policy Letter*, Summer 1996.

James A. Swartz, Arthur J. Lurigo, and Scott A. Slomka — "The Impact of IMPACT: An Assessment of the Effectiveness of a Jail-Based Treatment Program," *Crime & Delinquency*, October 1996.

Jeffrey Tauber — "Treating Drug-Using Offenders Through Sanctions, Incentives," *Corrections Today*, February 1994.

For Further Discussion

Chapter 1

1. Barry R. McCaffrey contends that illegal drug abuse has cost the United States over $300 billion and is responsible for 100,000 deaths since 1990. In contrast, Ethan A. Nadelmann argues that the escalation of the war on drugs in recent years has caused increases in drug-related death and crime. Based on your reading of these viewpoints, which of these perspectives has more merit? Which costs society more, drug abuse or the war on drugs itself? Defend your answer with references to the viewpoints.

2. According to Joseph D. McNamara, the law enforcement approach to the war on drugs is ineffective because the huge profits that can be made from selling illegal drugs makes it worth the risk of punishment. Robert E. Peterson, in contrast, cites statistics to support his argument that increased incarceration for drug offenses leads to a decrease in drug use and drug-related crime. Assuming Peterson's statistics to be valid, do you agree that putting more drug abusers in prison constitutes success in the war on drugs? Or do you agree with McNamara that other approaches are needed? Explain your answer.

3. William J. Bennett and his colleagues contend that recent increases in drug use can be reversed by a renewed emphasis on law enforcement and on education that stresses to teenagers the immorality of drug use. On the basis of the surveys of teenagers they cite, do you agree that teenage drug use can be decreased by the moral persuasion Bennett and his colleagues advocate? Why or why not?

Chapter 2

1. Richard Willard argues that federal policies on incarcerating drug offenders are too lenient and that more prisons and longer penalties for drug offenders are needed. David T. Courtwright, in contrast, maintains that the drug war strategy of incarceration is particularly harsh on black and minority drug offenders. Which author is more persuasive? Why?

2. Pamela Falk argues that the interdiction of drugs will significantly increase the cost of drugs, which will lead to a decrease in drug use. In contrast, Kenneth E. Sharpe contends that there is no evidence linking increased drug interdiction with lower drug prices or with decreases in drug use. Which view do you find more persuasive? Why?

3. Robert E. Peterson believes that drug education programs, such as the Drug Abuse Resistance Education (DARE) program, are effective in reducing drug use. D.M. Gorman, in contrast, asserts that "zero-tolerance" educational programs like DARE may actually be responsible for increased teenage drug use in recent years. Which of these views would appear to have common sense on its side? Which do you find more convincing? Why?

Chapter 3

1. Making a distinction between drug use and drug abuse, Benson B. Roe argues that many illegal drugs are not as physically harmful as they are portrayed to be. Robert L. DuPont contends that legalization will open the floodgates to increased abuse and addiction, creating a massive health care problem. Do you accept Roe's distinction between drug use and drug abuse, or do you agree with DuPont that there is only a thin line between the two behaviors? Defend your answer with reference to the viewpoints.

2. William J. Olson argues that advocates of drug legalization make false analogies when they compare use of illegal drugs with use of legal drugs like tobacco and alcohol. He argues that legalization would increase the health problems associated with drug use to levels comparable to the health costs associated with alcohol and tobacco use. In contrast, Steven B. Duke and Albert C. Gross suggest that legalization of drugs will result in a net reduction in health care costs as many people will switch from more harmful drugs, such as alcohol, to less harmful drugs, such as marijuana. Which argument do you find more persuasive? Why?

3. One problem faced by proponents of drug legalization is that of defining exactly what legalization would mean in practice. Would it mean all currently illegal drugs would be available to anyone over the counter? Or are restrictions possible, similar to those placed on the purchase and use of alcohol and tobacco? Which essays in this chapter advocate legalization, but with restrictions? What arguments against this position can you find in this chapter?

Chapter 4

1. Richard Brookhiser and Marcus Conant provide firsthand testimony that smoked marijuana provides medical benefits that no other drug can match. Dan Quayle, in contrast, cites the authority of several large medical groups that oppose legaliza-

tion of marijuana for medical purposes. Which kind of evidence do you find more persuasive, the firsthand testimony of the ill and those treating illnesses, or the authoritative judgment of large medical organizations? Explain your reasoning.

2. Most of the viewpoints in this chapter examine the controversy over the federally approved drug Marinol, which contains the active ingredient of marijuana in pill form. Is it inconsistent to endorse use of Marinol but to argue against the use of smoked marijuana for medical purposes? Or can Marinol have positive health benefits that smoked marijuana does not have? Find supporters of each position in this chapter. Which view is more convincing to you? Why?

3. Joseph A. Califano Jr. cautions states to approach legalization of medical marijuana slowly, comparing the rush for approval of marijuana to the approval of laetrile, which was eventually found to have no medical benefits in spite of anecdotal evidence. Is his argument convincing? Why or why not?

CHAPTER 5

1. In late 1996, Barry R. McCaffrey deliberately discussed the abuse of legal drugs such as alcohol and tobacco as a part of the war on drugs. Journalist Norman Solomon argues that this linkage is long overdue. Will this expansion of the war on drugs diminish the effectiveness of the prohibition message, in your view? Or is this a reasonable step to take in the war on drugs? Explain your answer.

2. Lisa Moore proposes that the war on drugs shift its priorities from the punishment of drug users to concern for the health and well-being of drug users. Is the harm reduction approach she advocates likely to win approval, in your view? What obstacles can you see in the way of such a proposal?

3. Michael Moline presents the case for drug courts that strive for the rehabilitation of drug offenders in place of harsher penalties wherever possible. Look carefully at the evidence he presents in support of this concept. Are you persuaded that these courts are successful, or do you have doubts about such rehabilitation efforts? Defend your answer with references to the evidence in this viewpoint.

ORGANIZATIONS TO CONTACT

The editors have compiled the following list of organizations concerned with the issues debated in this book. The descriptions are derived from materials provided by the organizations. All have publications or information available for interested readers. The list was compiled on the date of publication of the present volume; the information provided here may change. Be aware that many organizations take several weeks or longer to respond to inquiries, so allow as much time as possible.

American Council for Drug Education
164 W. 74th St., New York, NY 10023
(800) 488-DRUG (3784) • (212) 595-5810 ext. 7860
fax: (212) 595-2553
web address: http://www.acde.org

The American Council for Drug Education informs the public about the harmful effects of abusing drugs and alcohol. It publishes educational materials, reviews, and scientific findings and develops educational media campaigns. The council's pamphlets, monographs, films, and other teaching aids address educators, parents, physicians, and employees.

Canadian Centre on Substance Abuse (CCSA)
75 Albert St., Suite 300, Ottawa, ON K1P 5E7, CANADA
(613) 235-4048 • fax: (613) 235-8101
web address: http://www.ccsa.ca

CCSA works to minimize the harm associated with the use of alcohol, tobacco, and other drugs. It disseminates information on the nature, extent, and consequences of substance abuse; sponsors public debates on the topic; and supports organizations involved in substance abuse treatment, prevention, and educational programming. The center publishes the newsletter *Action News* six times a year, which can be ordered through e-mail at rgarlick@ccsa.ca.

Canadian Foundation for Drug Policy (CFDP)
70 MacDonald St., Ottawa, ON K2P 1H6, CANADA
(613) 236-1027 • fax: (613) 238-2891
e-mail: eoscapel@fox.nstn.ca
web address: http://fox.nstn.ca/~eoscapel/cfdp/cfdp.html

Founded by several of Canada's leading drug policy specialists, CFDP examines the objectives and consequences of Canada's drug laws and policies. When necessary, the foundation recommends alternatives that it believes would make Canada's drug policies more effective and humane. CFDP discusses drug policy issues with the Canadian government, media, and general public. It also disseminates educational materials and maintains a website.

Cato Institute

1000 Massachusetts Ave. NW, Washington, DC 20001-5403
(202) 842-0200 • fax: (202) 842-3490
e-mail: cato@cato.org • web address: http://www.cato.org

The institute, a public policy research foundation dedicated to limiting the control of government and to protecting individual liberty, strongly favors drug legalization. Its publications include the *Cato Journal*, published three times a year, and the bimonthly *Cato Policy Report*.

Center on Addiction and Substance Abuse (CASA)

Columbia University
152 W. 57th St., New York, NY 10019
(212) 841-5200 • fax: (212) 956-8020
web address: http://www.casacolumbia.org

CASA is a private, nonprofit organization that works to educate the public about the hazards of chemical dependency. The organization supports treatment as the best way to reduce chemical dependency. It produces publications describing the harmful effects of alcohol and drug addiction and effective ways to address the problem of substance abuse.

Drug Enforcement Administration (DEA)

700 Army Navy Dr., Arlington, VA 22202
(202) 307-1000
web address: http://www.usdoj.gov/deahome.htm

The DEA is the federal agency charged with enforcing the nation's drug laws. The agency concentrates on stopping the smuggling and distribution of narcotics in the United States and abroad. It publishes the *Drug Enforcement Magazine* three times a year.

Drug Policy Foundation

4455 Connecticut Ave. NW, Suite B-500, Washington, DC 20008-2328
(202) 537-5005 • fax: (202) 537-3007
web address: http://www.dpf.org

The foundation supports legalizing many drugs and increasing the number of treatment programs for addicts. The foundation's publications include the bimonthly *Drug Policy Letter* and the book *The Great Drug War*. It also distributes *Press Clips*, an annual compilation of newspaper articles on drug legalization issues, as well as legislative updates.

Drugs Data Center and Clearinghouse

PO Box 6000, Rockville, MD 20849-6000
(800) 851-3420 • (301) 519-5500
web address: http://www.ncjrs.org

The clearinghouse distributes the publications of the U.S. Department of Justice, the Drug Enforcement Administration, and other related federal agencies.

Heritage Foundation

214 Massachusetts Ave. NE, Washington, DC 20008-2302
(202) 546-4400 • fax: (202) 546-8328
web address: http://www.heritage.org

The Heritage Foundation is a conservative public policy research institute that opposes drug legalization and advocates strengthening law enforcement to stop drug abuse. It publishes position papers on a broad range of topics, including drug issues. Its regular publications include the monthly *Policy Review*, the Backgrounder series of occasional papers, and the Heritage Lectures series.

Libertarian Party

2600 Virginia Ave. NW, Suite B-100, Washington, DC 20037
(202) 543-1988
web address: http://www.lp.org/lp/

The Libertarian Party is a political party whose goal is to protect individual rights and liberties. It advocates the repeal of all laws prohibiting the production, sale, possession, or use of drugs. The party believes law enforcement should focus on preventing violent crimes against persons and property rather than on prosecuting people who use drugs. It publishes the bimonthly *Libertarian Party News* and periodic *Issues Papers* and distributes a compilation of articles supporting drug legalization.

Lindesmith Center

Soros Foundations/Open Society Institute
400 W. 59th St., 3rd Fl., New York, NY 10019
(212) 548-0181 • fax: (212) 548-4677
e-mail: lhallingby@sorosny.org
web address: http://www.lindesmith.org/

The Lindesmith Center is a policy research institute that focuses on broadening the debate on drug policy and related issues. The center houses a library and information center; organizes seminars and conferences; acts as a link between scholars, government, and the media; directs a grant program in central and eastern Europe; and undertakes projects on topics such as methadone policy reform and alternatives to drug testing in the workplace. The guiding principle of the center is harm reduction, an alternative approach to drug policy and treatment that focuses on minimizing the adverse effects of both drug use and prohibition. Particular attention is focused on analyzing the experiences of foreign countries in reducing drug-related harms. The center publishes fact sheets on topics such as needle and syringe availability, drug prohibition and the U.S. prison system, and drug education.

National Clearinghouse for Alcohol and Drug Information

PO Box 2345, Rockville, MD 20847-2345
(800) 729-6686 • (301) 468-2600 • fax: (301) 468-6433
web address: http://www.health.org

The clearinghouse distributes publications of the U.S. Department of Health and Human Services, the National Institute on Drug Abuse, and other federal agencies concerned with alcohol and drug abuse. Brochure titles include *Tips for Teens About Marijuana* and *Tips for Teens About Crack and Cocaine.*

National Council on Alcoholism and Drug Dependence (NCADD)
12 W. 21st St., 7th Fl., New York, NY 10010
(800) 622-2255 • (212) 206-6770 • fax: (212) 645-1690
web address: http://www.ncadd.org

The National Council on Alcoholism and Drug Dependence works to educate Americans about alcohol and drug abuse. It provides community-based prevention and education programs as well as information and service referrals. NCADD publishes pamphlets, fact sheets, and other materials that provide statistics on chemical dependency.

National Institute on Drug Abuse (NIDA)
U.S. Department of Health and Human Services
5600 Fishers Ln., Rockville, MD 20857
(301) 443-6245
e-mail: Information@lists.nida.nih.gov
web address: http://www.nida.nih.gov

NIDA supports and conducts research on drug abuse—including the yearly Monitoring the Future Survey—to improve addiction prevention, treatment, and policy efforts. It publishes the bimonthly *NIDA Notes* newsletter, the periodic *NIDA Capsules* fact sheets, and a catalog of research reports and public education materials such as *Marijuana: Facts for Teens.*

National Organization for the Reform of Marijuana Laws (NORML)
1001 Connecticut Ave. NW, Suite 710, Washington, DC 20036
(202) 483-5500 • fax: (202) 483-0057
e-mail: natlnorml@aol.com • web address: http://www.norml.org

NORML fights to legalize marijuana and to help those who have been convicted and sentenced for possessing or selling marijuana. In addition to pamphlets and position papers, it publishes the newsletter *Marijuana Highpoints*, the bimonthly *Legislative Bulletin* and *Freedom@NORML*, and the monthly *Potpourri.*

Office of National Drug Control Policy
Executive Office of the President
Drugs and Crime Clearinghouse
PO Box 6000, Rockville, MD 20849-6000

The Office of National Drug Control Policy is responsible for formulating the government's national drug strategy and the president's antidrug policy as well as coordinating the federal agencies responsible for stopping drug trafficking. Drug policy studies are available upon request.

RAND

Distribution Services

1700 Main St., PO Box 2138, Santa Monica, CA 90407-2138

(310) 451-7002 • fax: (310) 451-6915

web address: http://www.rand.org

The RAND Corporation is a research institution that seeks to improve public policy through research and analysis. RAND's Drug Policy Research Center publishes information on the costs, prevention, and treatment of alcohol and drug abuse as well as on trends in drug-law enforcement. Its extensive list of publications includes the book *Sealing the Borders* by Peter Reuter.

Reason Foundation

3415 S. Sepulveda Blvd., Suite 400, Los Angeles, CA 90034

(310) 391-2245 • fax: (310) 391-4395

e-mail: gpassantino@reason.org • web address: http://www.reason.org

This public policy organization researches contemporary social and political problems and promotes libertarian philosophy and free-market principles. It publishes the monthly *Reason* magazine, which contains articles and editorials critical of the war on drugs and smoking regulation.

BIBLIOGRAPHY OF BOOKS

Dan Baum — Smoke and Mirrors: The War on Drugs and the Politics of Failure. Boston: Little, Brown, 1996.

Ronald Bayer and Gerald M. Oppenheimer, eds. — Confronting Drug Policy: Illicit Drugs in a Free Society. New York: Cambridge University Press, 1993.

William J. Bennett, John J. DiIulio Jr., and John P. Walters — Body Count: Moral Poverty—and How to Win America's War Against Crime and Drugs. New York: Simon & Schuster, 1996.

Eva Bertram and Kenneth Sharpe — Drug War Politics: The Price of Denial. Berkeley and Los Angeles: University of California Press, 1996.

Vincent T. Bugliosi — The Phoenix Solution: Getting Serious About Winning America's Drug War. Beverly Hills, CA: Dove Books, 1996.

Robert C. Davis and Arthur Lurigio — Fighting Back: Neighborhood Antidrug Strategies. Thousand Oaks, CA: Sage, 1996.

Steven R. Donziger, ed. — The Real War on Crime: The Report of the National Criminal Justice Commission. New York: HarperCollins, 1996.

Steven B. Duke and Albert C. Gross — America's Longest War: Rethinking Our Tragic Crusade Against Drugs. New York: Jeremy P. Tarcher: Putnam Books, 1993.

Jeffrey M. Elliot — Drugs and American Society. Boston: Allyn & Bacon, 1994.

William N. Elwood — Rhetoric in the War on Drugs: The Triumphs and Tragedies of Public Relations. Westport, CT: Praeger, 1994.

Mathea Falco — The Making of a Drug-Free America: Programs That Work. New York: Random House, 1992.

Mathea Falco, ed. — Rethinking International Drug Control: New Directions for U.S. Policy. New York: Council on Foreign Relations, 1997.

H. Richard Friman — NarcoDiplomacy: Exporting the U.S. War on Drugs. Ithaca, NY: Cornell University Press, 1996.

Diana R. Gordon — The Return of the Dangerous Classes: Drug Prohibition and Policy Politics. New York: Norton, 1994.

Lester Grinspoon — Marijuana Reconsidered: The Most Thorough Evaluation of the Benefits and Dangers of Cannabis. Cambridge, MA: Harvard University Press, 1994.

Lester Grinspoon and James B. Bakalar — Marihuana: The Forbidden Medicine. New Haven, CT: Yale University Press, 1993.

Jill Jonnes — Hep Cats, Narcs, and Pipe Dreams: A History of America's Romance with Illegal Drugs. New York: Scribner, 1996.

Peter B. Kraska, ed.

Altered States of Mind: A Critical Observation of the Drug War. New York: Garland, 1993.

Richard Lawrence Miller

Drug Warriors and Their Prey: From Police Power to Police State. Westport, CT: Praeger, 1996.

Kenneth J. Meier

The Politics of Sin: Drugs, Alcohol, and Public Policy. Armonk, NY: M.E. Sharpe, 1994.

Philip P. Muisener

Understanding and Treating Adolescent Substance Abuse. Thousand Oaks, CA: Sage, 1994.

Office of National Drug Control Policy

Consult with America: A Look at How Americans View the Country's Drug Problem. Washington, DC: National Criminal Justice Reference Bureau, 1996.

Office of National Drug Control Policy

The National Drug Control Strategy, 1997. Washington, DC: Executive Office of the President, 1997.

Office of National Drug Control Policy

Pulse Check: National Trends in Drug Abuse. Washington, DC: Executive Office of the President, 1997.

Raphael F. Perl, ed.

Drugs and Foreign Policy: A Critical Review. Boulder, CO: Westview Press, 1994.

David A. Peters

The Probability of Addiction: Legal, Medical, and Social Implications. San Francisco: Austin & Winfield, 1997.

Craig Reinarman and Harry G. Levine, eds.

Crack in America: Demon Drugs and Social Justice. Berkeley and Los Angeles: University of California Press, 1997

Leif Rosenberger

America's Drug War Debacle. Brookfield, VT: Avebury, 1996.

Marc A. Schuckit

Educating Yourself About Alcohol and Drugs: A People's Primer. New York: Plenum, 1995.

Joseph Sora, ed.

Substance Abuse. New York: H.W. Wilson, 1997.

Paul B. Stares

Global Habit: The Drug Problem in a Borderless World. Washington, DC: Brookings Institute, 1996.

Arnold S. Trebach and James A. Inciardi

Legalize It? Debating American Drug Policy. Washington, DC: American University Press, 1993.

Theodore R. Vallance

Prohibition's Second Failure: The Quest for a Rational and Humane Drug Policy. Westport, CT: Praeger, 1993.

William O. Walker III

Drugs in the Western Hemisphere: An Odyssey of Cultures in Conflict. Wilmington, DE: Scholarly Resources, 1996.

Lynn Zimmer and John P. Morgan

Marijuana Myths; Marijuana Facts: A Review of the Scientific Evidence. New York: Lindesmith Center, 1997.

Franklin E. Zimring and Gordon Hawkins

The Search for Rational Drug Control. New York: Cambridge University Press, 1992.

INDEX